Charles Gamage Eastman

Poems of Charles G. Eastman

Charles Gamage Eastman
Poems of Charles G. Eastman
ISBN/EAN: 9783744704847
Printed in Europe, USA, Canada, Australia, Japan
Cover: Foto ©Thomas Meinert / pixelio.de

More available books at **www.hansebooks.com**

POEMS

OF

CHARLES G. EASTMAN.

MONTPELIER, VT.:
T. C. PHINNEY, PUBLISHER.
1880.

COPYRIGHTED BY
MRS. CHARLES G. EASTMAN,
MONTPELIER, VT.

WRIGHT & POTTER PRINTING COMPANY
18 POST OFFICE SQUARE, BOSTON, MASS.

CONTENTS.

Editor's Preface,	vii
Biographical Sketch of the Author,	xi
A Picture ("The Easy Chair"),	3
Purer than Snow,	4
Come Sing Me the Song,	5
The Late Season,	7
Of Love and Wine,	10
The Kidd-Man,	11
As Summer Fades away,	18
The Deformed,	19
A New Eugene Aram,	21
The Promise,	24
Dirge,	25
The Apple Blossom,	26
Love and the Poet,	27
The Haughty Maiden,	28
To Live upon Her Smile,	31
If You Think to Win Her,	32
Come over the Mountain to Me, Love,	33
Half My Life I Spent in Dreaming,	34
Sweetly She Sleeps,	35
Little Bel,	36
Mill May,	38
The Blind Beggar,	40
The Spring-Time,	42
A Wife-Song,	45
Twenty-Nine,	46
Shadows,	49
Lily,	51

EDITOR'S PREFACE.

IN presenting to the public this edition of the POEMS of CHARLES G. EASTMAN, its Editor deems it proper to make some explanation in regard to the many differences which will be noticed between the poems as here presented and in the edition of 1848. After publishing, Mr. Eastman, in an interleaved copy, was accustomed to often correct and change the readings of his poems, as his judgment or fancy at the time dictated; frequently not only altering the words, but the sense, of entire passages. He had also, before his sickness, entirely remodelled many of those poems which are generally regarded as his best. From this interleaved copy the present edition has been prepared. Wherever the alteration was *certainly intended* by the Author, it has been followed; but wherever the intention was doubtful, or the manuscript change was apparently made for the mere purpose of future adoption if finally approved, the original text has been restored. In these respects, the Editor has exercised, to some extent, his own discretion,— he trusts, not unwisely.

From among the unpublished manuscripts of Mr. Eastman, the Editor has selected, and presents in this edition, twenty-three new poems, and some fragmentary pieces which he deems too beautiful to be cast aside. Of these poems, two —" *The Old and New*," and the one we have entitled " *Life's Mission* " (the Author not having entitled it) — are of over five hundred lines each. These the reader may, properly perhaps, regard as unfinished and incomplete ; but from the fact that they were regarded by the Author as his most important work, and for the preservation of the many fine and finished passages they contain, we have chosen to include them in this volume. The manuscript of these poems when placed in our hands was in a most disorderly state. Written on loose sheets, without paging, it was embarrassed with numberless erasures, additions, and interlineations, and with duplicate and triplicate versions of the same passage, from which it was difficult to select the one approved by the Author, — to such an extent that the Editor has felt at times disposed, in distrust of his own power of proper arrangement, to discard them altogether. Having decided otherwise, influenced as much by the judgment of others as his own, it is hoped his errors may be pardoned. In these as in all other poems, the text of the Author has been scrupulously preserved.

The present edition has long been in contemplation, and has been anxiously expected by the Author's many admirers, but has been delayed by unavoidable circumstances. We take pleasure, at last, in presenting this volume of the Works of VERMONT's true POET.

G. R. T.

MONTPELIER, VT., Sept. 15, 1870.

THE Preface, as appears from the date, was prepared in 1870 by Mr. George R. Thompson, son of the late Hon. Daniel P. Thompson, of Montpelier.

Mr. Thompson was assisted in the preparation of this copy for the press by the Hon. Charles Reed, of Montpelier, a personal friend of Mr. Eastman; also, in the clerical labor, by Mr. Charles Loomis, of Montpelier.

Before the work was finally placed in the hands of the printer, all three of the above-named gentlemen passed from earth: hence a further delay has been the result.

The publication of the work is now undertaken, at the earnest request of a large circle of the admirers of Mr. Eastman, by loving friends.

M. D. G.

Montpelier, 1880.

BIOGRAPHICAL SKETCH OF THE AUTHOR.*

CHARLES GAMAGE EASTMAN was born at Fryeburg, Maine, June 1, 1816. His father, Benjamin C. Eastman, was by trade a watchmaker; and his mother was Rebecca Gamage, a woman beautiful in person, mind, and affections. At the early age of eleven years, tender in mind and fragile in body, young Eastman, with the independence which always characterized him, left his parental roof, and went out into the world; not choosing any longer to be a cause of expense to his parents, they being in humble pecuniary

---

* The writer of this has not intended or attempted to prepare more than a sketch of the life of Mr. Eastman, for the purposes of this edition of his Poems. It is to be hoped that his memoir will sometime be more adequately written. The writer, in the preparation of this paper, has availed himself greatly of the valuable biographical paper written on the occasion of Mr. Eastman's death, by his kinsman, Col. F. A. Eastman, of Chicago, Ill., and published in THE VERMONT PATRIOT, of Sept. 22, 1860.

circumstances. From that time forward he was the architect of his own fortunes. At the age of thirteen we find him attending school in the town of Windsor, Vermont; working his way as best he could, without uncompensated aid from any one. He made such progress in his studies that, the next year, he was successfully engaged in teaching school. Afterwards he continued his education at Meriden, N. H., where there was an excellent academical institution, and, having completed there his preparatory studies, at scarcely the age of eighteen he became a student at THE UNIVERSITY OF VERMONT, at Burlington. Here, to maintain himself, he made the usual shifts to which many young men resort. He taught, and he wrote for the newpapers; and here his attention was first turned to the profession — that of an editor — which, on leaving college, he adopted, and the exercise of which became the business of his life. His first newspaper enterprise was the starting of a small journal, in the interest of the Democratic party, at Johnson, Lamoille County, Vermont. This was not pecuniarily successful, though it attained some position and influence, and was abandoned. In 1840, not discouraged by this ill-fortune, Mr. Eastman fixed his residence at Woodstock, Vermont, where he inaugurated THE SPIRIT OF THE AGE; which newspaper at once assumed a high position among the organs of the Democratic party, and under his direction earned a reputation for energy, reliability, and strength. Mr. Eastman had, from his earliest manhood, been a zealous and consistent Democrat, embracing the principles of that party because sincerely convinced of their truth; and he gave to their promulgation and advocacy all his energy and ability. His mind soon became a leading one in the councils of his party in his adopted State, and he afterwards became a prominent director of its policy in national affairs. Seeking a wider scope for the exercise of his faculties, in 1846 he disposed of THE SPIRIT OF THE AGE, and purchased THE VERMONT PATRIOT, published at Montpelier, Vermont, then and now the leading Democratic organ of the State, in the editorship of which he continued until his death. It is as the conductor of this journal that he is the most widely remembered among politicians; and he managed it with an ability and faithfulness that secured it a reputation and influence seldom possessed by a country newspaper. His writings in this paper were

in accordance with the character of the man.—
direct, incisive, and earnest. He never hesitated
to say whatever was true, if it were proper to be
said; and in his exposures of the errors or frauds
of his opponents he employed intellectual weapons of the sharpest and most cutting kind. His
arguments were convincing, his logic clear, and
his convictions were stamped with truth. His
paper was not in any way pre-eminent as a literary
one. It might be supposed, judging from his almost idolatrous love of literary pursuits, that his
journal would have been more prominent in that
respect; but he never seemed ambitious to make
it so. These inclinations were gratified in another way. Though a member of a political party
never in the ascendancy in Vermont, he occupied
many influential official positions. He was a
leading member of the Democratic National Conventions of 1848, 1852, 1856, and 1860, and at
the time of his death was a prominent member of
the National Democratic Committee. In 1852
and 1853, he was a member of the Senate of the
State of Vermont, and a laborious and influential one; in which position he served with credit
to himself, and with advantage to the entire State,
as the prosperity of many of its most permanent

interests will attest. He was twice the popular candidate of his party for a seat in Congress and he was Postmaster at Montpelier nearly six years.

At the time he fixed his residence at Montpelier, he married Mrs. Susan S. Havens, daughter of Dr. John D. Powers, of Woodstock, Vermont, who now survives him. [The fruit of this union was two sons (both now deceased) and a daughter; the latter, Mary Avery Eastman, is a native of Montpelier, where she was born in 1849; in 1872 she married Eldin J. Hartshorn, a son of Hon. John W. Hartshorn, of Lunenburg, Vermont. Mr. and Mrs. Hartshorn, immediately after their marriage, settled at the present city of Emmetsburg, Palo Alto County, Iowa, where they still reside.

Mr. Hartshorn is a lawyer by profession, having read law at Rutland, Vermont, in the office of Messrs. Veazey and Dunton.

Mr. Hartshorn was a member of the House of Representatives of Iowa two years, and has just entered upon his second term as a State senator from his district; he is also mayor of his adopted city.

Mr. and Mrs. Hartshorn have three children living, having lost one.

Mrs. Eastman continues to reside in Montpelier, although she passes a portion of each year with her daughter.]

Mr. Eastman died at his residence in Montpelier, Sept. 16, 1860. From the preceding May, a disease of the most obstinate and painful character had burdened his spirit and wasted his frame. Faithful to the complicated interests with which he was identified, and the responsibilities that had accumulated upon him, he unwisely, but most unselfishly (as was like him), made secondary his own interests of health and life. His pride and sympathies were enlisted in the business of his party, and he did what he thought to be his duty. But he was at home in the bosom of his family when his eyes closed to the scenes he loved so well; and his last moments, painless and calm, were brightened by the love of family and friends, and cheered with the substantial hope of eternal happiness and joy.

In person Mr. Eastman was large and strong, well-formed, and with a face of remarkable beauty. He possessed one of those faces which involuntarily attract,—one which at once excited admiration and respect. Though frequently he seemed rapt and abstracted, and withdrawn within himself, at other times every feature became mobile with life and gayety. He would seem, at times, in his thoughts to wander far away from the scenes around him, and his mind would seek its enjoyment elsewhere; but as often he would enter into the spirit of the hour, with a glee boyish and almost boisterous. Long by those who knew him will his genial face and contagious laugh be remembered. Especially was he the friend of the young. No young man, doubtful and hesitating in his first venture in life, ever sought encouragement from him in vain, or left him without a brighter hope. Little children loved him; and he had ever a pleasant word for them. For them, as for all, his smile was most kindly and winning. They, the best judges of us all, well knew he was generous, sympathetic, and humane. In his own family his life was lovely. It is well described in the words of Rev. Dr. William H. Lord spoken at his funeral to his mourning family, now proved prophetic:—

"You will remember him first and longest for what he was to you personally,— for what he was in his domestic and social relations. You will not forget the kindness of his heart, the amenity and cheerfulness of his manners, the liveliness of fancy and wit with which he cheered the household. .... You will not lose the recollection of his kind words, of his considerate attentions, of his fatherly acts and affections. You will remember the melody of his flute, as it led the voices of his children in their songs and hymns; the written prayers, which I am told he composed for them, to be used morning and evening in their devotions. And so long as love has a place in your hearts, this household will not cease to have a shrine where his memory shall be kept green and sacred."

Many incidents, illustrative of the character of Mr. Eastman; of his kindness and generosity; of his hatred and contempt of wrong, and his true sense of justice; of his pure wit and lively fancy; of his impatience of bigotry and cant, and his reverence for all things truly good and truly sacred; of his broad and liberal views of life, and his charity for thoughtless or repented erring; of his true poetic appreciation of beauty in things animate and inanimate, — crowd upon our memory; but the purposes of this sketch forbid us to indulge in their relation here. May his heart and soul find a fitting portraiture by an abler and more accurate hand!

Mr. Eastman, from his college days to the day of his death, devoted more or less of his time to the indulgence and expression of his poetic feelings; and he is best known and will be longest remembered by his poetic works. He was rapid and fluent in composition, but most laborious and fastidious in revision, perhaps too much so. He would vary the expression of his idea *ad infinitum* almost, and never seemed to think anything he wrote could not be improved. When his poems were given to the public, he was exceedingly sensitive and doubtful as to their reception; and, when the book appeared, was almost sorry he had published it. Its success was at once assured, and his position as a poet of great merit at once allowed. In this country and in Europe his writings have received the highest commendation. As a lyrical poet, there is no American writer who can be called his superior; hardly any one his equal. Aside from the finish and delicacy of expression, the natural and easy mingling of sentiment and description, the chief charm of his poetry is its perfect *truth*. Every New-England reader will recognize in his descriptive pieces many a perfect reproduction of the incidents and scenes of his boyhood. His words and expressions are those in common use, simple and expressive; and his subjects are at once understood, and his allusions appreciated. "Why," once said Mr. Eastman to the writer, "do they talk about the yew and the myrtle? Why don't they write about the spruce and the hemlock, the maple and the butternut? We don't have any yew-trees in this country." Mr. Eastman's pieces descriptive of local scenery and manners are among his best. There is hardly a Vermont man who does not know well "The Old Pine-Tree," or who is not very well acquainted with "Uncle Jerry." Many of us have looked upon the "Scene in a Vermont Winter," though perhaps without its melancholy incident. Mr. Eastman handled these subjects with such perfect truth of description that they are almost unsurpassed.

His lyrics are exceedingly musical. One reads many of them with the involuntary impression that, instead, he ought to *sing* them. But in his compositions the poetry equals and sometimes surpasses the music. His songs are of very unequal merit, and this inequality sometimes extends to different parts of the same piece. Those that are humorous, or are characteristic of manners, copy nature no less than those that are descriptive. Those that are serious and general are tender and sweetly interesting. In these latter Mr. Eastman exhibited the great sensibility of his heart, no less than his understanding, and these will be found to infuse the living principle into all the works of genius which are destined to immortality. His sensibility had an uncommon range. He was alive to all emotion; and he has reared a fair and enduring monument of his genius.

T.

NOTE. — That part of the above sketch inclosed in brackets, on pp. xv, xvi, has been added since the death of Mr. Thompson.

PART I.

A PICTURE.

The farmer sat in his easy chair
    Smoking his pipe of clay,
While his hale old wife with busy care
    Was clearing the dinner away;
A sweet little girl with fine blue eyes
On her grandfather's knee was catching flies.

The old man laid his hand on her head,
    With a tear on his wrinkled face,
He thought how often her mother, dead,
    Used to sit in the self-same place;
As the tear stole down from his half-shut eye,
"Don't smoke!" said the child, "how it makes
    you cry!"

The house-dog lay, stretched out on the floor
    Where the shade after noon used to steal,
The busy old wife by the open door
    Was turning the spinning-wheel,
And the old brass clock on the mantletree
Had plodded along to almost three.

Still the farmer sat in his easy chair,
    While close to his heaving breast
The moistened brow and the cheek so fair
    Of his sweet grandchild were pressed;
His head, bent down, on her soft hair lay:
Fast asleep were they both, that summer day!

PURER THAN SNOW.

Purer than snow
Is a girl I know;
Purer than snow is she;
Her heart is light,
And her cheek is bright. —
Ah! who do you think she can be?

I know very well,
But I never shall tell,
'Twould spoil all the fun, you see;
Her eye is blue;
And her lip, like dew,
And red as a mulberry.

Mild as a dove
Is a girl I love;
Mild as a dove is she;
And dearer, too,
Than ten like you. —
Ah! who *do* you think she can be?

COME SING ME THE SONG.

Come sing me the song that you sang years ago,
 When we sat by the soft-flowing brook,
With the lilies we'd picked from the bank, in each
 hand,
 And the light of first love in each look.
Though the clover has faded, and withered the
 flowers,
 That our forms in that summer day pressed,
And more loves than one in each bosom have
 been
 Since then a too well cherished guest;
  Yet, sing me the song that you sang years ago,
   When we sat by the soft-flowing brook,
  With the lilies we'd picked from the bank, in
   each hand,
   And the light of first love in each look.

Come sing me the song that you sang years ago,
 When your cheek like the morning was fair,
When the sweet-elder blow and the strawberry
 vine
 I twined in the curls of your hair.
Though your cheek has grown pale, and my hair
 has grown gray,
 And your lip lost its mulberry red,

And the thousand bright hopes that we talked
 over then,
 Like the passion that nursed them, have fled ;
*Yet, sing me the song that you sang years ago,
 When we sat by the soft-flowing brook,
 With the lilies we'd picked from the bank, in
 each hand,
 And the light of first love in each look.*

THE LATE SEASON.

The skies are clouded, and the hail
   Drives at the window all the day ;
And, through the gloomy evening, wail
   Uneasy winds along the way ;
No herald of the promised flowers
   Above the cheerless plain appears ;
And April's cold, ungenial showers
   Fall to the earth like frozen tears.

With freezing nights and days o'ercast,
   Stern Winter! still thy reign is here,
To vex the husbandman, and blast
   The promise of the opening year.
And though the month is far behind
   When shouting troops of children deck
The lusty Aries, and bind
   The wreath about his snowy neck ;

Still thou art building o'er the streams
   The agile skater's glassy floor,
And shaping in the moon's cold beams
   Fantastic shadows, while the roar
Of dismal winds is heard at night
   Upon the mountain, and, below,
The valley still is cold and white,
   And cheerless with the drifting snow.

How long shall bud and blossom wait
    For thy departure? It is time
To hear the whippoorwill, the prate
    Of birds about their nests, the chime
Of running waters by the way,
    The busy swallows at the eaves,
And soft-winged zephyrs out at play
    Among the grass and growing leaves.

The seed is waiting for the plough,
    While o'er his wet and dreary land
The husbandman, with gloomy brow,
    Sees still the frozen waters stand;
And as, with stinted measure, he
    Doles the last labors of the flail,
Doubts if he have not lived to see
    The seed-time and the harvest fail.

Mark how, sometimes, 'tis seen that Wrong
    Will scowl upon the dawning light!
And gathering up his knotted thong
    Will scourge and buffet back the Right!
But mark how soon, o'er all the earth,
    His last black day of hate is won!
And Time's full travail with the birth
    Of radiant Truth comes surely on!

So thou shall have thy day, stern child
    Of tempests! soon, thy frosty locks
Shorn from thy brow by zephyrs mild,
    Shalt thou depart, and grazing flocks

Shall crop the grass the clouded sun
    Has checked awhile ; in summer hours
Above thy grave shall children run,
    And wreath their hair with gathered flowers.

Lo! southward, where the horizon's verge
    Sinks its blue circle from the eye,
Where still the burly tempests urge
    Their fierce authority, the sky
With milder hue begins to glow,
    And clouds, that in the atmosphere
Bosom soft gales and rain-drops, grow
    Blushful with the returning year.

Not long can seasons late, or storms
    Keep back the seed-time, and the grain,
That Nature in her bosom warms,
    Shall, in its own due time, again
Put forth the promised blade ; and though
    Untimely frosts and rains delay
The ear, yet shall the full corn grow
    And ripen for the harvest day.

OF LOVE AND WINE.

Of love and wine old poets sung,
    Old poets rich and rare, —
Of wine with red and ruby heart,
    And love with golden hair;
Of wine that winged the poet's thought,
    And woke the slumbering lyre;
Of love that through the poet's line
    Ran like a flash of fire.

But wine, when those old poets sung
    Its praises long ago,
Was something subtler than the bards
    Of modern ages know; —
Ay, wine was wine when Teian girls,
    Flushed with the rosy dew,
To old Anacreon's fiery strains
    Through wanton dances flew.

And love, when those old poets sung
    Its praises long ago,
Was something warmer than the bards
    Of modern ages know; —
Ay, love was love when Teian girls,
    Flushed with the melting fire,
With roses crowned Anacreon's brow,
    With kisses paid his lyre.

THE KIDD-MAN.

TELL you a story! Alice dear,
　　I'm afraid you have asked in vain!
Since your mother died, in your second year,
I've forgotten all that I knew, I fear;
And the stories I told when she was here,
　　I can never repeat again.

But yet, perhaps, as it is not late, —
　　And here by my watch I see
The hands point six on the dial-plate, —
I'll try if before they are round to eight
My fancy fail of her wonted gait,
　　And this shall the story be : —

I.

An old man lives, as the story goes,
　　In a hut, just out of the town,
Where under the hill the hemlock grows,
Shading till June the winter snows,
And a living springlet bubbling flows
　　From a rock in the mountain brown.

The queerest man that was ever on earth,
　　And a very queer man is he,
Nobody knows who gave him birth;

He never sits down at any man's hearth,
And he seems to think of very small worth
What was, or what is to be.

II.

And how does he look? why, Alice, his skin
Is withered, and brown as tea,
And the wrinkles so thick that the point of a pin
Anywhere on his face, a wrinkle were in! —
Stooping and short, meagre and thin,
And hands that reach to his knee.

In his eyes there shines, it is plain to see,
A disordered and feverish will;
As far in his head as they well can be,
They're as blue as you ever saw blue-berry,
But dreamy and deep, as though infancy
Were wondering through them still.

His hair is white as the falling snow,
But silky and soft as a girl's;
And falling far down his shoulders below,
Like a patriarch's seen in a picture, you know,
Streams round his neck in the winds as they
    blow,
In a thousand beautiful curls.

III.

But his beard is short, and blacker than jet.
And it never was shaved, they say;
And his teeth, through his lips, you can see, are set

Closely together, as though they met
To crush the remembrance, lingering yet,
  Of things that have long passed away.

Through summer and spring, when the skies are
    fair,
  He scarce ever goes out of the door;
But sits at his hearth, with his dog by his chair,
And the smoke of his pipe wreathes round in his
    hair,
As he crosses his legs with a thinking air,
  Or wanders about the floor.

IV.

But they say, when the sky with a tempest
    scowls,
  And the lightning flares and gleams,
When the raving wind through the cavern
    prowls,
And over the peaks of the mountain howls,
And, with long and low intonations, growls
  The distant thunder, he seems

Like a man at the top of his element,
  In the midst of the deafening roar —
Shouts as the hemlock-trees are bent!
And the oak by the bolt is torn and rent!
And laughs as the riven leaves are sent
  Like feathers about his door!

V.

And they say, he'll stand and turn his ear,
   And the peals count one by one,
As the cloud sweeps onward, black and near,
And the bolts fall fast, distinct and clear,
As though each clap that he turns to hear
   Were the burst of a battle gun.

There is something, 'twould seem, in summer bright
   That he always seeks to shun;
And 'tis said that he utterly hates the light,
That the leaves and the flowers annoy his sight,
That he only can bear the half-day-night
   Of the gloomiest winter sun.

VI.

But as soon as the days grow short and dim,
   And the mountain is covered with snow, —
When the trees look ghastly, bare, and grim,
And the sleet clings closely to trunk and limb,
And the rivers are frozen from brim to brim,
   And the sun to the south runs low, —

Then the old fellow's out! and you never will find
   Another so strange and queer; —
His cap is of coon, with the red-fox lined,
Like a bee-hive shaped, with the tail behind,
That flaps o'er his back in the saucy wind,
   'Twould make you laugh for a year.

VII.

His horse is a poor and a sorry old lout,
    And a sorry old lout is he ;
His head hangs down, and his bones stick out,
And he scarcely can turn the old pung about,
And he cares not a pin for the street-boy's shout,
    Or his master's gee-up ! gee !

The harness is shabby and old, alack !
    A rope and a strap and a thong ! —
There's a cord for the reins, and a piece of sack
Doubled up for a pad, on the old horse's back,
While the trace-chains jingle a-whick-a-ty-whack !
    Round the thills as he shuffles along.

VIII.

O'er his shoulder he holds, of the blue-beech green,
    A long, sturdy twig, for a whip,
And, as forward a little you see him lean,
He uses it often and well, I ween ;
For thick and large, and plain to be seen,
    Are its marks on the old horse's hip.

Behind him follows, led by a twine,
    His beautiful dog, Bessie ;
Her hair is curly and black and fine,
And parts along on her back in a line,
And glossy and bright, in the clear sunshine,
    As a fully-ripe blackberry.

IX.

So he rides along from street to street,
 Turning that way and this ;
He minds not a soul he may chance to meet,
He never looks up from his horse's feet,
And cares not a straw for the hail and sleet
 That beats in his face, I wis.

And though the wind's up, and the snow is whirled
 So that nobody else can see,
You'd think, as his whip round his head is twirled,
And the puffs of smoke from his stub pipe curled
Through his jetty black beard, that he owned the new world,
 And a part of the old countrie!

X.

Most terrible tales are about him told,
 And I've heard our grandmother say,
She'd no doubt, in his hut, he had chests full of gold,
For which to old Nick his soul he had sold;
That he always had been just about so old
 Since he first came along this way.

XI.

'Tis sure, no doubt, the old fellow must be
 As old as the oldest crow ;
But whether he's sold to the devil, is he.

Whether he has murdered folks on the sea,
Or whether he's wicked or very godly,
   Nobody pretends to know.

XII.

But you know there was once a Captain Kidd,
   You have heard, I am sure, of him!
The man of the song, who " so wickedly did,"
Who all in the sand the Bible hid!
And the laws of God to his crew forbid, —
   A pirate, bloody and grim!

And this crazy and foolish old man, you see,
   So close in his hut keeps hid
That the gossips insist there is some mystery
About him, and sagely declare it must be,
So strange are his ways and his doings, that he
   Is some such a fellow as Kidd!

XIII.

And so it is now, wherever he goes,
   Sorry to say am I!
Every child in the street the old man knows,
And whether it shines or whether it snows,
Whether it rains or whether it blows,
   " THE KIDD-MAN!" is the cry.

AS SUMMER FADES AWAY.

Ah, me! the sky is dark and cold,
　　The leaves are dead and gray,
And everything seems growing old
　　As summer fades away;
The clouds along the valley drift,
　　Or round the mountain run,
Too heavy with the rain to lift
　　Their bosoms to the sun.

I hear upon the frozen grass
　　The cold and dripping rain,
And mark the shadows as they pass
　　Along the cheerless plain;
See one by one the flowers, across
　　The dreary fields, depart;
And of old age the sullen moss
　　Feel growing o'er my heart!

Ah, me! the sky is dark and cold,
　　And sharp and keen the storm,
That cuts, as though my blood were old,
　　My pinched and shivering form;
The vigor from my blood has fled,
　　My brain seems in decay,
And everything looks dark and dead
　　As summer fades away.

THE DEFORMED.

She was not beautiful, poor girl!
   Her figure or her face
Had none of all the charms that give
   To maidenhood its grace;
A gentle being, on whose heart
   All sorrows seem to fall;
Deformed and homely, poor and sad,
   And mind to feel it all!

They shunned her at our village sports,
   And, when the gay and fair
Were gathered at the festival,
   I never found her there.
They knew the poor and homely girl
   Had little art to speak
Where fashion's bold and glaring lights
   Were blazing on her cheek.

And, never asking look or word
   To cheer the lonely hours,
She sought no sympathy beyond
   Her mother and her flowers.
Her shrinking soul could never brook
   The haughty eye of pride;
And, hardly known beyond her door,
   She lived and wept and died.

At last, beneath December's snow,
  The few that knew her well
Went out and laid the girl to rest;
  And now there's none can tell
Where bloom the clover white and red
  That Nature kindly rears
To guard her slumbers, weary child
  Of poverty and tears.

A NEW EUGENE ARAM.

He cannot flee it! — since the night
   His murderous hand was laid
Upon the weary traveller,
   Far in the lonely glade,
That face he saw, upturned and pale,
   A moment in the light
The setting moon gave through the pines,
   Has never left his sight.

The Magi's page, the mystic arts
   Of men who've sought to tell
Our strange and hidden destiny
   By star and crucible;
The thoughts of those who've dared to search
   The dark and the unknown, —
Who've watched the secret springs of life, —
   For years he made his own.

He stood upon the Appenines;
   Where famed Lepanto swells,
And where Marmora heaves her heart
   Along the Dardanelles;
Where, round her cold and ice-bound capes,
   The freezing Arctic sweeps;
Where still above her perished bride
   The Adriatic weeps;

Amid her ruins who was once
    The mistress of the world;
Where for the banner of the cross
    The battle-axe was hurled;
Upon the hallowed mount where erst
    The God of Abram spoke;
And on the hill where fabled Jove
    His wrathful thunders broke;

On Asia's sands, where silence rules
    With unmolested reign;
Beneath the Moslem minaret;
    Beside the Pagan fane;
Where Egypt's pyramids record
    Traditions dark and dim:
Yet, like a Presence was that face
    Forever unto him.

It haunts him in the forest shade,
    It haunts him where the roar
Of rushing multitudes is like
    The sea upon the shore;
It haunts him in the blaze of day,
    And when on Ida's steeps
Her watch above her lover-boy
    The fabled huntress keeps.

He cannot flee it: from the pines
    Where shone the moonlight dim
The night the weary traveller died,
    That pale face followed him;

And evermore the pallid brow,
   Marked by the crimson spot
Between the locks of fallen hair,
   Where struck the cursed shot;

And ever the half-conscious eyes,
   The dark blow on the cheek,
The pale lips parted with a prayer
   They moved in vain to speak, —
Are with him as they were the night
   His murderous hand was laid
Upon the weary traveller,
   Far in the lonely glade.

THE PROMISE.

I showed my love a budding rose,
   And bade the girl beware!
Believe, I said, as summer flowers
   Our youthful pleasures are;
And love is like the bud we see,
   Whose heart will soon be blown,
Most fragrant when its leaves are fresh,
   Ere one soft tint has flown.

And she, with sweet and bashful eye,
   Her face half from me turned
In soft confusion, as I spoke,
   My meaning well discerned;
And promised, when the bud I saw
   Should open to the sky,
That she my full desire, at last,
   No longer would deny.

DIRGE.

Softly!
  She is lying
    With her lips apart;
Softly!
  She is dying
    Of a broken heart.

Whisper!
  Life is growing
    Dim within her breast;
Whisper!
  She is going
    To her final rest.

Gently!
  She is sleeping,
    She has breathed her last!
Gently!
  While you're weeping
    She to heaven has passed.

THE APPLE BLOSSOM.

Here's an apple blossom, Mary;
  See how delicate and fair!
Here's an apple blossom, Mary;
  Let me weave it in your hair!

Ah! thy hair is raven, Mary,
  And the curls are thick and bright;
And this apple blossom, Mary,
  Is so beautifully white!

There! the apple blossom, Mary,
  Looks so sweet among your curls!
And the apple blossom, Mary,
  Crowns the sweetest of the girls.

But the apple blossom, Mary,
  You must have a little care
Not to tell your mother, Mary,
  That *I* wove it in your hair!

LOVE AND THE POET.

In his chamber sits the Poet,
  Beats his heart with feelings dim,
Love is there! but who should know it?—
  Scarcely is it known to him.

Visions indistinct and shifting
  Pass before his half-shut eye,
Like the idle clouds that, drifting,
  Laze along the summer sky.

But the visions, ever taking
  Forms of beauty rare and bright,
In the Poet's heart are waking
  Indefinable delight.

Time went on, the visions slowly
  Take a shape of rarest life!
And the Poet's heart so lowly
  Beats with a tumultuous strife.

Love, at last, with gentle power,
  Opens in the Poet's heart,
Like the unfolding of a flower
  When its leaves are blown apart.

In his chamber sits the Poet,
  Flit no more the shadows dim:
Love is his, and all may know it,
  Well I ween 'tis known to him!

THE HAUGHTY MAIDEN.

The maiden sat beside the brook,
And gazed upon the sky,
The summer wind the maple shook,
The stream went rippling by.
A noble youth before her stood,
And prayed with earnest tone,
By all of earth 'twas fair and good,
That she would be his own.
    But still the maiden's haughty look
    Was bent upon the sky,
    And still the wind the maple shook,
    And still the stream went by.

A thousand earnest things he said
To win her cruel ear, —
She only bent her stately head
To show that she could hear.
With hand upon his manly breast —
For he could not give o'er —
He urged again, again he pressed
What he had urged before.
    But still the maiden's haughty look
    Was bent upon the sky,
    And still the wind the maple shook,
    And still the stream went by.

He spoke of heart and feelings wrung,
    Of doubts and hopes and fears ;
He told her how his heart had clung
    To hope and her for years ;
How, wandering in a foreign land,
    For her an exile, he
Had met her face upon the sand,
    Her image on the sea.
        But still the maiden's haughty look
            Was bent upon the sky,
        And still the wind the maple shook,
            And still the stream went by.

And then, at last, his eye grew dark,
    And pallid grew his face,
And on his forehead came the mark
    That slighted love will trace.
He turned and left the maiden's side,
    Nor word of parting spoke,
But passed with strong and rapid stride
    Beyond the ancient oak.
        Yet still the maiden's haughty look
            Was bent upon the sky,
        And still the wind the maple shook,
            And still the stream went by.

And years went on ; he came no more
    To see the haughty maid ;
His first wild dream of love was o'er,
    And in oblivion laid ;

He passed into the world and grew
A strong one in the land,
A man with pulse and effort true,
And never-failing hand.
> And still the maid whose haughty look
> Was bent upon the sky
> In summer sits beside the brook,
> And sees the stream go by.

TO LIVE UPON HER SMILE.

To live upon her smile, methinks
    It were an idle pain;
To burn beneath her eye, methinks
    It were to burn in vain,—
If still she runs and still is coy,
And still refuse the promised joy.

To gaze upon her lip, methinks
    It were of little use;
To see and never taste, methinks
    It were a mean abuse,—
If still she runs and still she flies,
And still puts off and still denies.

To talk of what may be, methinks
    Were vainly spending breath;
To feed on hope too long, methinks
    Were starving one to death,—
If still she runs, and still will say,
" Ah, ha! ah, ha! another day!"

IF YOU THINK TO WIN HER.

Do you think to win her
 With a bashful tongue?
Fie! thou green beginner,
 You are still too young!
Looks that shun her glances,
 To her feet that go,
Make but poor advances,
 Seeking what's so low.

Love that asks no pressing,
 Knows no daring mood,
Yearns for no caressing,
 Dies for want of food.
Better seek to win her
 With a bold constraint;
Better be a sinner,
 Than a bashful saint.

COME OVER THE MOUNTAIN TO ME, LOVE.

Come over the mountain to me, love,
 Over to me;
My spirit is pining for thee, love, —
 Pining for thee.
SWEET April is here, and the buds
 On the elms are beginning to swell,
The meadows look green, and the flowers
 Are blossoming up in the dell:
'Tis the time when you promised, you know, love,
 To return to your lover, again;
When the robins came back, and the snow, love,
 Had melted away from the plain.

Come over the mountain to me, love,
 Over to me;
My spirit is pining for thee, love,—
 Pining for thee.
A robin was here, yestermorn,
 And the leaves of the lilac appear;
The martins around their old nests,
 We soon from the window shall hear;
'Tis the time when you promised, you know, love,
 You'd return to your lover again;
When the robins came back, and the snow, love,
 Had melted away from the plain.

HALF MY LIFE I SPENT IN DREAMING.

HALF my life I spent in dreaming
　Of a love I dare not speak,
In sweet imagination, deeming
　That I lived upon her cheek.
And, while I saw her beauty wasting
　By the silent flight of years,
Consoled myself with fancied tasting,
　Lulled with dreams my rising fears.

And when, at last, my heart no longer
　Satisfied with seeming good,
Sought, as its pulse grown older, stronger,
　For a more substantial food, —
I found, too late, the vain Ideal
　Living in my snowy head
Cherished, till, alas! the Real
　In my heart was cold and dead.

SWEETLY SHE SLEEPS.

Sweetly she sleeps! her cheek so fair
  Soft on the pillow pressed.
Sweetly, see! while her Saxon hair
  Watches her heaving breast.
Hush! all low, thou moving breeze,
  Breathe through her curtain white;
Golden birds, on the maple-trees,
  Let her sleep while her dreams are light.

Sweetly she sleeps, her cheek so fair
  Soft on her white arm pressed.
Sweetly, see! and her childish care
  Flies from her quiet rest.
Hush! the earliest rays of light
  Their wings in the blue sea dip.
Let her sleep, sweet child, with her dreams so bright,
  And the smile that bewilders her lip.

LITTLE BEL.

THREE summers with their blossoms fair
  Have on her being smiled, —
How glossy is her waving hair!
  How beautiful the child!
Pray look a moment in her eye,
  So like the blue of yonder sky!

She is an orphan, Little Bel,
  With strangers hath she grown;
Mary mother, shield her well!
  'Tis hard to be alone.
She hath no kindred on the earth:
Her mother perished at her birth.

She knows it not; yet something brings
  The tears into her eye,
As closer to my heart she clings,
  She cannot tell me why, —
As though to win by such caress
Protection for the motherless.

And sometimes in her talk she'll stop
  Beside her cradle-place.
Her playthings from her fingers drop,
  And, looking in my face,
Her thoughts seem in her heart to stir
As though some mystery troubled her.

And sometimes our dear mother's name
  She speaketh sad and slow,
As though to her 'twere not the same, —
  And yet she cannot know, —
She sleepeth on the same fond breast
That all of us in childhood pressed.

It may be, while the orphan sleeps,
  So sinless she and mild,
Her mother's angel spirit keeps
  Communion with her child;
That in her dreams she vaguely learns
The loss of that for which she yearns.

MILL MAY.

The strawberries grow in the mowing, Mill May,
And the bob-o'-link sings on the tree,
On the knolls the red clover is growing, Mill May,
Then come to the meadow with me!
We'll pick the ripe clusters among the deep grass
On the knolls in the mowing, Mill May,
And the long afternoon together we'll pass
Where the clover is growing, Mill May.

Come! come ere the season is over, Mill May,
To the fields where the strawberries grow,
While the thick-growing stems and the clover, Mill May,
Shall meet us wherever we go;
We'll pick the ripe clusters among the deep grass
On the knolls in the mowing, Mill May,
And the long afternoon together we'll pass
Where the clover is growing, Mill May.

The sun, stealing under your bonnet, Mill May,
  Shall kiss a soft glow to your face,
And your lip, the strawberry leave on it, Mill May,
  A tint that the sea-shell would grace;
Then come! the ripe clusters among the deep grass
  We'll pick in the mowing, Mill May,
And the long afternoon together we'll pass
  Where the clover is growing, Mill May.

THE BLIND BEGGAR.

HE sits by the great high-road all day,
   The beggar blind and old;
The locks on his brow are thin and gray,
   And his lips are blue and cold;
The life of the beggar is almost spent,
His cheek is pale and his form is bent,
And he answers low and with meek content
   The sneers of the rude and bold.

All day by the road has the beggar sat,
   Weary and faint and dry,
In silence, patiently holding his hat
   And turning his sightless eye,
As, with cruel jest and greeting grim
At his hollow cheek and eye-ball dim,
The traveller tosses a cent at him,
   And passes hastily by.

To himself the blind old man doth hum
   A song of his boyhood's day,
While his lean, white fingers idly drum
   On his thread-bare knee where they lay;
But oft when the gay bob-o'-link is heard,
And the robin's chirp to the yellow bird,
The jar of life and the traveller's word,
   And the noise of the children's play,

He starts as he grasps with a trembling hand
    The top of his smooth-worn cane,
And strikes it sturdily into the sand —
    Then layeth it down again ;
While his black little spaniel, beautiful Spring,
That he keeps at his button-hole with a string,
Jumps up, and his bell goes ting-a-ling ! ling !
    As he yelps at the idle train.

He sits by the great high-road all day,
    The beggar blind and old ;
The locks on his brow are thin and gray,
    And his lips are blue and cold ;
Yet he murmurs never, day nor night,
But, seeing the world by his inner sight,
He patiently waits with a heart all light
    Till the sum of his life shall be told.

THE SPRING-TIME.

The earth is green again. The upshooting blade
 Pierces the sullen mould, and from its bed
The flower, where round the forest springs were
 made
The paths in summer, lifts its timorous head;
And clouds, that hang above the narrow glade,
 O'erladen with the gushing rain they shed
In generous bounty, crowd the hill and plain
With greener grass and swelling buds again.

No more at morn the sharp and cutting gales
 The watchful husbandman with sorrow fill;
No more at night the hollow tempest wails,
 Nor sweeps at noon the blast along the hill;
And save the drifts that in the mountain vales
 Stretch their huge forms, defying still
The sunlight, and the ice that to the rocks
Clings, dripping underneath the cold hemlocks,

No mark is left to tell of Winter's reign, —
 Of cheerless mornings and of lengthened night;
And, sloping downward to the blue Champlain,
 Lie the smooth meadows, level, green, and
 bright;
And, crowded to their tops with sprouting grain,
 The noble highlands stretch beyond the sight;
While waving trees, with leaves all fresh and green,
Glance far the mountain valleys up between.

Behold! In vain the stern North-west defies
  The genial influence of the ascending sun,
That, circling up the broad, benignant skies,
  With vigorous heat begins to run
His summer circle ; and the gales that rise,
  And breathe upon the fields, grown sere and dun
With snows untimely and with frosts severe,
Herald the triumph of the coming year.

Through all the day, along the valley blows
  The warm and wooing zephyr. O'er the plain,
With measured bounty, cheerful labor sows
  The broken tillage with the hopeful grain ;
Along the pastured hills and woodland, flows
  The brook, full-swollen with the snow and rain ;
And gloomy fears no more to all the land
Presage a harvest with an empty hand.

Distrustful, faithless man ! But yesterday
  Thy fields were viewed with dark and sullen brow
And murmuring, as the chilling snow-drifts lay
  Above the frozen furrows of the plough, —
The sunshine and the fruitful showers of May,
  The promised seed-time and the harvest, thou
Half questioned if His power again renew ! —
And now the gales are warm and skies are blue,

And all thy seeds are cherished ; on the hill
    Thy teeming flocks again the pastures try,
And vigorous sons go forth at dawn to till
    Thy meadow-lands beneath a cheerful sky.
Renewing all her beauties, Nature still
    Spreads out the landscape to thy gladdened eye :
On every hand the buds of promise start,
To chide thy fretful lip and murmuring heart.

Let spring-time, now returning, teach thee, friend !
    For, lo ! up-rising ever by thy way
Assurances, where'er thy footsteps tend,
    That Life shall always triumph o'er Decay, —
Teach thee more faithful trust, unto the end,
    In Him who quickeneth the silent clay,
And from the mouldering darkness of the tomb
Renews the promise of unfading bloom.

A WIFE-SONG.

I touch my harp for one to me
    Of all the world most dear,
Whose heart is like the golden sheaves
    That crown the ripened year;
Whose cheek is fairer than the sky
    When 't blushes into morn,
Whose voice was in the summer night
    Of silver streamlets born;—

To one whose eye the brightest star
    Might for a sister own,
Upon whose lip the honey-bee
    Might build her waxen throne;
Whose breath is like the air that woos
    The buds in April hours,
That stirs within the dreamy heart
    A sense of opening flowers.

I touch my harp for one to me
    Of all the world most dear,
Whose heart is like the clustering vine
    That crowns the ripened year;
Whose love is like the living springs
    The mountain travellers taste,
That stormy winter cannot chill,
    Nor thirsty summer waste.

TWENTY-NINE.

WITH singing birds and growing leaves,
    With budding flower and vine,
My birth-day morning dawns again,
    And I am twenty-nine.
And Time, although some marks appear
    By which his flight I trace,
Most kindly with my heart has dealt,
    And kindly with my face.

And if 'twere not, as I look back
    Along the years I've run,
And through them trace the winding path
    That I have slowly won;
Or mark the graves where sleep, alas!
    So many loved and near,
Who in the stern life-battle fell,
    Who, lost, are yet more dear;

And that the ghosts of hopes and fears
    That shook my younger heart,
Unbidden, will sometimes into
    The light of memory start, —

But little there were left to tell
  That I am older now
Than when a laughing boy I ran
  To kiss my mother's brow.

So soft has been the tread of Time,
  Like children's feet on snow;
So quietly the years have passed,
  And still so calmly go, —
'Twere wrong for me to murmur, while
  I scrawl this foolish line,
That dawns my birth-day morn again,
  And I am twenty-nine.

It is no idle thing to live!
  And he who clearly sees
The thousand snares that haunt his life, —
  Sin, accident, disease;
Who marks how he escapes this ill
  By slightest circumstance,
And hardly grasps that passing good
  By mere and rarest chance;

Who notes his whole existence changed,
  Even sometimes by a dream, —
His fortune warped by incidents
  Most trivial that seem, —
Will start to find how near his feet,
  In ignorance, have shaped
His path along some peril's brink
  That he has barely 'scaped.

A fearful thing to live! and when
  My slender bark has passed
Thus safely by the rapids, where
  So many wrecks are cast,
I look upon my life, and find,
  Upon the record set,
More cause for joy and thankfulness
  Than sorrow or regret.

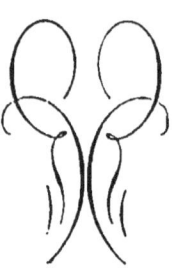

SHADOWS.

How they come and go,
Shadows on the snow!
Coming ever,
Going ever;
Rapidly they shift
Over plain and drift,
Leaving where they were
Nothing but the air.
See them! as a cloud,
Slowly, like a shroud,
Folds the darkened moon,
At its noon.

How they run and quiver,
Shadows on the river!
Coming ever,
Going ever;
Flitting o'er the stream,
Like the memory of a dream,
Leaving not a trace
On its quiet face.
See them! as a cloud,
Slowly, like a shroud,
Moves across the sun,
Mid-day won.

Come they and depart,
Shadows o'er the heart —
　　Coming ever,
　　Going ever. —
Wherefore, who can tell?
Indefinable!
Dim and dark they pass,
Like vapor o'er a glass.
　　　　See them! as a cloud,
　　　　Slowly, like a shroud,
　　　　Settles on the heart,
　　　　　　To depart.

How they gather nigh,
Shadows o'er the eye!
　　Coming ever,
　　Going never!
Gathering o'er the strife
Of departing life,
Leaving in a breath
The mystery of death.
　　　　See them! as a cloud,
　　　　Slowly, like a shroud,
　　　　Passes o'er the light —
　　　　　　It is night!

LILY.*

Tell me, pretty Lily,
    With your lips apart,
Here among the lilacs,
    Have you found a heart?

Mine, I cannot find it,
    Searching in the dew,
Sure I am I lost it,
    Playing here with you.

Lily! have you found it?
    Cruel! ah, I see!—
Pity a poor rhymer!
    Give it back to me!

Away the beauty bounded,
    Laughing as she flew;
My heart, among the lilacs,
    From her bosom threw.

Glad I seized it, hidden
    In a rose half blown,
Lily! careless Lily!
    Ah, it was her own!

---

* The reader of the former edition of "Eastman's Poems" will hardly recognize these rhymes. It is proper to state that, after its original publication, the Author prepared many other versions, in a selection from which the Editor has followed his own judgment.— Ed.

I SEE HER NOT!

I SEE her not! the spring is here
    With gladness for the budding earth;
I see her not! the one so dear,
    Nor at the board, nor at the hearth;
The dust is on her window-sill,
    Her bird is dumb, her flowers are dead,
And, in the fastened shutter, still
    The spider weaves her gloomy thread.

Here, in her silent chamber, where
    The solitary shadows dwell,
I watched, with sweet and patient care,
    The sister I had loved so well;
And when a day of sharper pain
    Had left her hopeless, pale, and weak,
I sought to cheer her heart again,
    And kiss the color to her cheek.

Here, through the long, long winter night,
    She wore the weary hours away,
Until at last the morning light
    Came through her window cold and gray;
Ah, how the dull beam on the glass
    Would still to her the hope restore,
That she the leaves and growing grass
    Might live to look upon, once more!

I could not tell her what, to learn,
    Would only needless anguish give,
That spring to her would ne'er return ;
    For on that hope she seemed to live :
She could not, so she'd come to think,
    She could not sleep beneath the snow ;
Yet, as each day I saw her sink,
    I knew too well it must be so.

And so it was : but yet, her breath
    So quietly one morn was stilled,
While yet that hope was strong, that death
    To her was but that hope fulfilled ;
For, hours before her spirit passed,
    Sweet names of flowers her lips would spell,
And, murmuring faintly, " Spring at last ! "
    Upon her face the shadow fell.

I see her not ! the spring is here !
    And gladness reigns through all the earth ;
I see her not ! the one so dear,
    Nor at the board, nor at the hearth ;
The dust is on her window-sill,
    Her bird is dumb, her flowers are dead,
And, in the fastened shutter, still
    The spider weaves her gloomy thread.

PRAYERS FOR A SICK CHILD.

I.

SPARE the sufferer, cruel Pain!
    Spare the child!
Let her breathe in sleep again,
    Calm and mild.
All our hopes are centred here,
And we pray with many a tear,
    Spare the child!

She hath never injured aught
    'Neath the sun!
Pure is she as Love's first thought, —
    Gentle one!
Ah! we cannot bear the fear
That her life must vanish here,
    Just begun.

Spare the sufferer, cruel Pain!
    Spare the child!
Let her breathe in sleep again,
    Calm and mild.
For ourselves we've little fear —
For the suffering angel, hear!
    Spare the child!

II.

Vainly we have striven,
    And our skill is o'er;
Aid the child thou'st given!
    We can do no more.
Ah, the moan it utters!
    It can take no rest;
And the low breath flutters
    Faintly from its breast.

We have no ambition,
    We're a humble pair,
Seeking no condition
    Save our lot of care;
We have murmured never, —
    Unto labor wed, —
But with chaste endeavor
    Sought our daily bread.

This poor child we cherish,
    That thy mercy gave;
Father! shall it perish?
    It is all we have!
Bid the burning fever
    The gentle sufferer spare!
A little longer leave her
    To our humble care!

ISABEL.

Are thy thoughts upon the sea,
    Isabel?
Are thy thoughts upon the sea,
    Isabel?
    All day sitting,
    Thinking, knitting,
Scarcely ever looking slyly up as formerly at me ;
    Where's thy chatter?
    What's the matter,
    Isabel?

Are thy thoughts upon the sea,
    Isabel?
With a lover on the sea,
    Isabel?
    Poor aunt Lizzy
    Was *so* dizzy
When the symptoms made appearance of this
    maiden malady !
    And the labors
    Of the neighbors,
    Isabel !

Are thy thoughts upon the sea,
    Isabel?
With " that fellow " on the sea.
    Isabel?

That poor hoddy —
That nobody ! —
Have you ever seen him noticed by the first
society ?
Mind thy mother !
Love another,
Isabel !

Are thy thoughts upon the sea,
Isabel ?
Are they still upon the sea ? —
Isabel ?
Hear thy betters !
Burn his letters !
Let thy very kind relations make a proper match
for thee ;
Cash and station, —
Rich relation, —
Isabel !

If thy heart is on the sea,
Isabel,
And thy thoughts are on the sea,
It is well !
Round thy lover
Let them hover,
Though thy mother says Old Skinflint has more
mortgages than he ;
Thy lip's honey
Sold for money, —
Isabel !

HOW CALMLY PASS HER QUIET DAYS.

How calmly pass her quiet days
   In womanly repose!
As sometimes by the dusty ways
   A stream, half-hidden, flows,
So softly that the traveller's ear
Scarce hears its current bubbling near.

Most beautiful, yet never proud;
   Beloved, yet never vain;
Though courteous to the idle crowd
   That come and go again,
Yet happiest when her time is spent
With those she loves in calm content.

She knows but little of the art
   By which we learn the right:
Her knowledge lieth in her heart,
   In woman's keen insight;
And much she teaches by her looks
That we could never find in books.

With patient grace she moves along
   Through all her duties; oft
Beguiling them with sweetest song,
   And chastened mirth and soft;
And all the day, like some sweet bird,
The music of her voice is heard.

Long may she live! see clearer still,
　With ever-brightening eye,
And learn serenely to fulfil
　Her woman-destiny;
And happier, purer, grow each day,
As steals her quiet life away.

NAY, MOTHER! TELL ME NOT.

Nay, mother! tell me not that he
    Is lost to virtue yet,
Though well I know ten thousand snares
    His youthful feet beset.
And, mother! well I know that you
    His dearest hopes have crossed,
And now, when he has fallen, cry,
    I told you! — he is lost!

I know him, mother, and I know
    How much you hate that boy!
But it shall prove, though you despise,
    You never can destroy!
He loves me, mother, and for that
    These snares his feet beset;
And, mother, though the world combine,
    That love shall save him yet!

SHE PERISHED ERE HER HEART HAD KNOWN.

She perished ere her heart had known
  A sorrow or a fear,
Ere o'er her spirit care had thrown
  A shadow, — Mary, dear!
And life to her was like a gleam
Of sunshine on a valley stream.

She sleeps beneath a rising hill
  That looks upon the West ;
Dead to the world, but living still
  To those who knew her best :
And on her grave, with folded wings,
The sober blue-bird sits and sings.

We miss her ; she was dear ; we miss
  Her laugh at eventide,
Her fondling arms, her gentle kiss.
  But yet, 'tis well ! — she died
All pure and bright as at her birth, —
A gain to heaven, a loss to earth.

WE WEEP IN VAIN.

We weep in vain; the book is shut —
    The fountain sealed — and there!
The one we loved so much is but
    The dust of hopes that were!
The eye is closed, the ear is dull,
Alas, alas! so beautiful!

We weep in vain: above her head,
    With all its golden wealth,
Steeped in our tears, the pall is spread —
    So young, so full of health! —
Ah! who that met her yesternoon
Had dreamed to see her thus, so soon?

We weep in vain: there! let her sleep
    Beneath the maple-tree;
The stars above her grave will keep
    Their vigils; — sadly we
Return to life, with many a tear,
And one tie less to bind us here.

SONG IN AUTUMN.

Take down the sickle, boys! hurrah!
    The ears of ripened grain
Are waiting for the reaper's hand,
    Upon the fruitful plain!
The mellow moon, the changing leaves,
    The earlier setting sun,
Proclaim at last, my merry boys,
    The harvest-time begun.

Thick on the hills, to-morrow noon
    The gathered stook must see,
And with the loads of yellow corn
    Shall groan the axle-tree;
The frost, my boys, will soon be here!
    And winter's on the way; —
These glorious days will never, boys,
    For lazy farmers stay!

Take down the sickle, boys! hurrah!
    While loads of ripened grain
Are waiting for the reaper's hand,
    Upon the fruitful plain,
We'll gather up the golden corn
    In thankfulness, once more,
And fill with the returning seed
    Our basket and our store.

HER GRAVE IS BY HER MOTHER'S.

HER grave is by her mother's,
    Where the strawberries grow wild,
And there they've slept for many a year, —
    The mother and the child.

She was the frailest of us all,
    And from her mother's breast
We hoped and prayed and trembled more
    For her than all the rest.

So frail, alas! she could not bear
    The gentle breath of spring,
That scarce the yellow butterfly
    Felt underneath its wing.

How hard we strove to save her, love
    Like ours alone can tell;
And only those know what we lost
    Who've loved the lost as well.

Some thirteen summers from her birth,
    When the reaper cuts the grain,
We laid her in the silent grave,
    A flower without a stain.

We laid her by her mother,
    Where the strawberries grow wild,
And there they sleep together, —
    The mother and the child.

SHE REIGNETH IN THIS HEART OF MINE.

She reigneth in this heart of mine,
   My beautiful, my own!
She reigneth in this heart of mine,
   A queen upon her throne;
And I, a poor and humble man,
Yield to her rule as best I can.

She reigneth in this heart of mine,
   By night, and all the day
She reigneth in this heart of mine;
   And I have naught to say,
Save, now and then, to sigh, " Ah, me!
Was ever such harsh tyranny?"

She reigneth in this heart of mine,
   All rivalry hath flown;
She reigneth in this heart of mine
   Despotic and alone.
I strove awhile against the chain;
But I shall never strive again!

She reigneth in this heart of mine,
   A queen upon her throne;
She reigneth in this heart of mine
   As though it were her own.
So long a slave, I cannot tell
If to be free were now as well.

SHE LIVETH BY THE VALLEY BROOK.

She liveth by the valley brook,
    Away from care and wrong,
Her heart a pure and open book,
    Her lip a mellow song.
A mother, meek and old, is all
    The kindred that she knows;
Her playmates are the waterfall,
    And every flower that blows.

She singeth when the earth is spread
    With green, and spring has come;
And weepeth when the flowers are dead,
    And her sweet brook is dumb.
And thus the gentle maiden's life
    Steals quietly away,
Without a shade of care or strife
    To cloud its summer day.

She liveth by the valley brook,
    Away from care and wrong,
Her heart a pure and open book,
    Her lip a mellow song.
Ah, never may the maiden dream
    Of this sad world of ours,
Or stray beyond her sister stream,
    Its valley and its flowers!

MARY OF THE GLEN.

Has anybody spoke for you,
  Mary of the Glen?
Is there a heart that's broke for you,
  Mary of the Glen?
I have lands and I have leases,
  I have gold and cattle, too,
I have sheep with finest fleeces —
  Can I marry you?

Nobody, sir, has spoke for me,
  Mary of the Glen;
There is no heart that's broke for me,
  Mary of the Glen;
But there is blue-eyed Willie,
  Who labors with the men,
Who brings the sweet pond-lily
  To Mary of the Glen!

He has neither lands nor leases;
  But his cheek is cherry red,
And finer than your fleeces
  Are the curls upon his head.
    And though he's never spoke for me,
      I know he loves me true;
    And his heart it would be broke for me,
      If I should marry you.

I BLAME THEE NOT!

I BLAME thee not! — I knew it all
    Before a glance from thee
Could stir my heart as doth the wind
    The slumber of the sea;
I knew, before thy presence made
    Of this fair life a part,
Another, many a year, had been
    The idol of thy heart.

I never strove to check a love
    So hopeless and so bright,
Like some sweet star the school-boy sees
    In the far heavens at night;
And though at times there came a thought
    That I was wronging thee,
I could not quench that star myself,
    For it was life to me.

I never wished to steal a look
    Or thought of thine from him;
I would not for the world have seen
    His worshipped light grow dim;
I never meant to let thee know —
    God grant I never did! —
That in my heart I nursed for thee
    A love by love forbid.

So — hoping without hope — I loved;
　Too blest to think how fast
The hour was stealing on me when
　I *must* awake — 'tis past!
The fault was mine — I knew it all —
　And yet, despite this pain,
As I have loved, I dare not say
　I should not love again.

Well! Southern suns will soon renew
　Thy cheek's half-perished health,
While he — God bless him! — proudly shares
　Thy heart's long-treasured wealth;
The bark that bears thee from the North,
　With sails set for the sea,
Is fading on the misty main. —
　Good-bye to that and thee!

EVENING IN SUMMER.

The sun has set at last! the sky,
   That all the hot and stifling day
Hung like a burning arch on high,
   Grows, as the fierce heat dies away,
Cool and refreshing; o'er the glades
   The hills frown giant-like and grim;
And meadows, in the misty shades
   Of night, look shadowy and dim.

The sun is down; yet, in the West
   Is lingering still the day's last light
Around the hills his glory blest
   When sinking slowly from the sight;
And, far above the mountain brown,
   Along the dreamy azure, sleep
The small, white clouds, like tufts of down
   Upon the bosom of the deep.

As twilight fades, how all the earth
   The night with solemn gladness fills!
The moon, as fair as at her birth,
   Where heaven is wedded to the hills
Through fleecy clouds around her flung,
   Wheels up beside the same sweet star,
That, with her, when the sky was young,
   Looked over Eden from afar.

Beneath the moon the wild brook learns
  Its own sweet music; o'er the plain,
The tired husbandman returns
  Rejoicing to his home again;
While, from the dense old forest-trees,
  Where, shrouded from the scorching heat,
All day it slept, the evening breeze
  Comes sweeping up the dusty street;

And, passing on its mission, goes
  To cool the parched and fevered soil,
To bless the fainting vine that throws
  Its tendrils round the door of toil,
And stir the myriad leaves, until
  Their rising murmur swells along
With all life's utterances, that fill
  The world with a perpetual song.

MARY BLANE.

Here's a health to thee, Mary Blane!
Here's a health to thee, Mary Blane!
Here's a health to the girl that I loved when a boy,
   Though I never shall see her again.
'Tis right to remember old friends;
   'Till well, is it not, Mary Blane,
When the heart's growing old and the blood's
   . getting cold,
   To live our first love o'er again?
     Hurrah for thee, Mary Blane!
     Hurrah for thee, Mary Blane!
     Hurrah for the girl that I loved when a boy,
       Though I never shall see her again!

Here's health to thee, Mary Blane!
Here's health to thee, Mary Blane!
To thee, wherever thou art, Mary Blane,
   This full glass of sherry I drain.
'Twas a sweet little time that we had,
   A nice little time, Mary Blane!
And with sorrow I think, while I scribble and
   drink,
   We shall see no more like it again!
     Hurrah for thee, Mary Blane!
     Here's a health to thee, Mary Blane!
     Though the wine that I drink, in my head,
       Mary Blane,
     Like thy love in my heart, leave a pain!

I'VE THROWN THEM ALL AWAY!

I'VE thrown them all away! away!
  And not a single token
Is left me to recall the day
  His fickle vows were spoken.
The scarf he o'er my shoulders threw,
  The ring (his name was on it),
His card, the flowers, the *billet-doux*,
  The warm and flattering sonnet, —
      Away! away!
  I've thrown them all away!

I've thrown them all away! away!
  And brightly on the morrow
Will beam the eye that yesterday
  Was dimmed an hour with sorrow.
The chain, the lute, the singing-bird,
  The books he used to bring me,
The letters which my tears have blurred,
  The songs he used to sing me, —
      Away! away!
  I've thrown them all away!

I've thrown them all away! away!
All thoughts of the false-hearted.
And now my heart's as wild and gay
As though we'd never parted;
　The glow is on my cheek again,
　And every idle token
He left me to recall the pain
　Of vows so falsely spoken, —
　　　Away! away!
I've thrown them all away!

THE TOWN PAUPER'S BURIAL.

BURY him there —
No matter where!
Hustle him out of the way!
Trouble enough
We have with such stuff —
Taxes and money to pay.

Bury him there —
No matter where!
Off in some corner at best!
No need of stones
Above his old bones —
Nobody'll ask where they rest.

Bury him there —
No matter where!
None by his death are bereft;
Stopping to pray? —
Shovel away!
We still have enough of them left.

Bury him there —
No matter where!
Anywhere out of the way!
Trouble enough
We have with such stuff —
Taxes and money to pay.

THE REAPER.

BENDING o'er his sickle,
    Mid the yellow grain,
Lo, the sturdy reaper,
    Reaping on the plain!
Singing as the sickle
    Gathers to his hand,
Rustling in its ripeness,
    The glory of his land.

Mark the grain before him
    Swaying in the wind,
See the even gavel
    Following behind!
Bound, in armful bundles,
    Standing one by one,
Yester-morning's labor
    Ripens in the sun.

Long I've stood and pondered,
    Gazing from the hill,
While the sturdy reaper
    Sung and labored still;
Bending o'er his sickle,
    Mid the yellow grain,
Happy and contented,
    Reaping on the plain;

And as upon my journey
   I leave the maple-tree,
Thinking of the difference
   Between the man and me,
I turn again to see him
   Reaping on the plain,
And almost wish *my* labor
   Were the sickle and the grain.

I WOULD THAT HE WERE BACK!

I would that he were back again,
　From lands beyond the sea!
I cannot bear to hear them say,
　"He will be false to thee!"
I know 'tis childish — idle — weak —
　I know 'tis wrong in me;
But yet, I would that he were back,
　From lands beyond the sea.

I would that he were back again!
　While he is far away,
They breathe their slanders in my ear
　Through all the weary day;
He's harsh, they say, and proud and cold,
　That one beyond the sea;
He may be so to them, perhaps,
　He never was to me.

I would that he were back again,
　To crush this servile throng!
One glance from his indignant eye —
　Why is he gone so long?
Oh! if he knew how I have borne,
　As none but Heaven knows,
The doubtings of his fickle friends,
　The insults of his foes!

I would that he were back again!
'Tis hard to hear them say,
Ambition or another's love
Prolongs his weary stay.
I fear him not! his love is true!
And yet, though weak in me,
I would that he were back again,
From lands beyond the sea!

THANATOS.

I.

Hush! her face is chill,
    And the summer blossom,
Motionless and still,
    Lies upon her bosom;
On the shroud so white,
    Like snow in winter weather,
Her marble hands unite
    Quietly together.

II.

Ah, how light the lid
    On the thin cheek presses!
Still her neck is hid
    By her golden tresses;
And the lips, that Death
    Left a smile to sever,
Part to woo the breath
    Gone, alas! forever.

FANNY HALL.

The sweetest girl of all I know
   Is charming Fanny Hall;
The wildest at a husking,
   The gayest at a ball;
Her cheek is like a Jersey peach,
   Her eye is blue and clear,
And her lip is like the sumac
   In the autumn of the year.

Canova never made a hand
   Like hers so plump and fair;
Poor Raphael had been crazed with her
   Madonna brow and hair;
And I'm inclined to think if Powers
   Could see her, he would grieve
To find a romping Yankee girl
   Had beaten Mrs. Eve!

There's not a blemish in her form,
   No fault about her face.
Sit down and gaze from morn till night —
   You'll find her perfect grace.
And then, to finish all, her voice!
   From the sweetest bird's in spring
You couldn't tell its warble; but
   She " doesn't know a thing!"

APRIL RAIN.

I.

GENTLY fall upon the plain
April rain!
  Bless the oak and maple bud,
  Rouse the faint and sickly flood;
But the gentle flowers,
  Tender leaf and blow,
Ah! the heavy showers,
  Kill them where they grow.

II.

Do thy mission on the plain
April rain!
  Bless the grass and apple bud,
  Cheer the faint and sickly flood;
But the gentle flower,
  On the meadow's breast,
Spare its little hour,
  Short enough at best!

MUTABILITY.

Alas, how soon the heart forgets
    Its wildest, deepest pain!
A tear an hour the eyelid wets,
    And all is joy again!
Still rushes on the tide of men
As though the past had never been.

A year, one year, is scarcely gone,
    Since, in the dreary fall,
We heaped the frozen clay upon
    The dearest of us all;
And now, alas! as 'twere a dream
The memory of that day doth seem.

She was our life but yestermorn,
    And by her tombstone now
We sing and plant the yellow corn,
    And drive the furrowing plough,
As gay as though beneath that stone
Were sleeping one we'd never known.

OLD TIME STEALS ON.

Old Time steals on, and away he goes!
Away he goes, goes he;
He stealeth away, and nobody knows
Whence cometh or goeth he.
He lingereth never for rich or for poor,
For palace or hovel, for prince or for boor;
O'er the grave and the cradle he glideth along,
And alike amid sorrow, alike amid song,
Old Time steals on, and away he goes!
Away he goes, goes he;
He stealeth away, and nobody knows
Whence cometh or goeth he.

From youth to age, how quick is his flight!
From night to morn, from morning to night!
And hurrying on in his own silent way,
Mid the snows of December, the blossoms of May,
Old Time steals on, and away he goes!
Away he goes, goes he;
He stealeth away, and nobody knows
Whence cometh or goeth he.

For war or for peace, for loss or for gain,
For love and for hate, for pleasure or pain,
For grace or dishonor, for glory or shame,
Not a moment he tarries; but, ever the same,

Old Time steals on, and away he goes!
Away he goes, goes he;
He stealeth away, and nobody knows
Whence cometh or goeth he.

Well! since it is settled that this is the way
Old Time dashes on with us, day after day,
Sweet girls! while in handfuls we pile on his wing
The soft, dewy roses of Love, let us sing
Old Time steals on, and away he goes!
Away he goes, goes he;
He stealeth away, and nobody knows
Whence cometh or goeth he.

SHE IS THE LAST!

She is the last of all that God
   Has given to our hearth;
Two brothers sleep beneath the sod —
   They perished at their birth;
Ah! fondly did we hope that she
Would live through her frail infancy.

She is the last, and there she lies!
   Beneath the locust-tree
We've laid to rest, with streaming eyes,
   The last of all the three;
We've heaped the clay above her breast,
And left her sleeping with the rest.

She is the last: we give her up
   With silent lips to Heaven.
Submissively we take the cup, —
   'Tis bitter, but 'tis given:
And, trusting still in Him who gave,
We yield our last hope to the grave.

THE UNKNOWN SLEEPER.

Beneath an aged locust-tree
 Upon the blue Lamoille,
Where, all the summer day, the bee
 Sings at her busy toil,
By brake and grass and vine o'ergrown,
A child's unlettered grave is shown.

None know how long the sod has been
 Above the sleeper's breast,
And none can tell the stranger when
 The child was laid to rest;
No kindred has it left to tell
Its birth, its death, or burial.

Long, long ago, they'll tell you, when
 The deer came there to drink,
Before a hut in all the glen
 Stood on the river's brink,
A hunter in his wanderings found
The locust and the gentle mound.

And since, though sire and son, the land
 Have tilled with thrifty care,
Yet all have let the locust stand,
 And still the grave is there,
Beside the river on the plain
Of waving grass and yellow grain.

About the mound they've built a pale
    Of rude and artless form,
Through which the bending meadow-swale
    Sighs in the autumn storm;
And where their young the ground birds feed
Among the grass and yellow weed.

As 'twere their own, that nameless child,
    They watch its long repose
Beneath the brake and brier wild,
    The strawberry and the rose;
And every spring an hour they save
To mend the pale that guards the grave.

LOOKING IN THE RIVER.

Looking in the river,
    Smiling to herself,
Sits a little maiden
    On a mossy shelf;
Looking in the river,
    What's the maiden see?
Than herself, I'm certain,
    Something it must be!

Looking in the river,
    Where the shimmering sun,
Than the orb above her
    Seems another one;
Looking in the river,
    There the maiden sees
Something than the heavens,
    Or the mirrored trees!

Looking in the river
    With a dreamy stare,
Wonder what the maiden
    Can be seeing there?
Looking in the river,
    What if *I* should be?
Then I may be certain
    What the girl can see.

Looking in the river —
Now, ah, ha! I know
What the little maiden
Gazes at below!
Looking in the river,
Now I understand
Why the little maiden
Sits upon the land!

Looking in the river,
As the water stirs,
There I see another
Face look up with hers!
Looking in the river,
Close beside her own,
There I see another
Face in shadow thrown.

Looking in the river,
Just behind the maid,
There I see her lover
In the maple shade!
Looking in the river,
Now I understand
Why the little maiden
Sits upon the land!

Looking in the river
With her other self,
Sits the little maiden
On a rocky shelf;

Looking in the river, —
Maiden, never run!
That's a thing I'm certain
All of us have done.

Looking in the river!
All of us have been,
And can tell the summer
We remember, when,
Looking in the river,
By the shadow thrown,
We have seen another
Face beside our own.

NOVEMBER.

The days we've so long dreaded,
　The days of frost and snow,
Of winds that sweep the frozen street,
　And whistle as they go —
The days of fickle temperament,
　A smile and then a blow!
Of mud and mire and dirtiness, —
　Again, are "here below"!

We sit and sneeze and cough in rooms
　Insufferably hot,
And tumble over old accounts
　Were never worth a groat!
And, looking from the window
　Into our neighbor's lot,
We really argue if 'twere best
　To steal his sheep or not!

The vines, frost-bitten, from the eaves
　Hang blackening in the rain;
And trickling drops, like silent tears,
　All day the windows stain;
The leaves are gone, the dead weed-stalks
　Grow black upon the plain,
And herds are lowing in the fields
　Where stood the gathered grain.

All day you hear the noisy crow
    Upon the hemlock high;
In flocks, about the mountain ash,
    The chirping robins fly;
The rustling leaves drive waywardly
    In mimic whirlwinds by,
Or on the wet and muddy walks,
    In heaps, together lie.

The dripping of the rain is heard
    Upon the roof all night,
And dark and heavy clouds obscure
    The early morning's light:
We gape and stretch, and feel as dull
    As our grandmother's sight,
" Some " older than Methuselah,
    And cross enough to bite!

That summer's gone, and gone for good,
    'Tis useless to protest,
When all the hills that you can see,
    In snowy caps are dressed;
When fogs upon the valley
    From morn till evening rest,
And in his journey scarce the sun
    Is seen from east to west.

Alas! these days of dumps and of
    Interminable rains,
Of overcoats and overshoes,
    And 'pothecary grains, —

Of drops for coughs, and slops for colds,
From catnip tea to Swayne's, —
Make the effort to survive appear
A questionable pains!

SONG

"Bring me a cup, — a brimming cup!
Bubbling with rosy, red wine;
For, soon as the blossoms of summer shall bud,
Sweet Alice has sworn to be mine.
    Joy! joy!
Sweet Alice has sworn to be mine!"

"But women are gay, and light as the air,
As faithless as faithless can be;
And their love is as fickle and as false as the moon,
The wind, or the waves of the sea!
    Drink, boy!
But Alice will never be thine!"

"Bring me a cup, — a brimming cup!
Laughing with rosy, red wine;
For women are true as the sun,
And Alice has sworn to be mine!
    Joy! joy!
And Alice has sworn to be mine!"

"A gallant I saw at her feet but now,
I swear by this goblet of wine!
And he said, as he pressed her lip to his own,
Sweet Alice has sworn to be *mine!*
    Drink, boy!
But Alice will never be thine!"

"Bring me a cup, — a brimming cup!
  Laughing with rosy, red wine;
For women are true, and thou liest, I know,
  For Alice has sworn to be mine!
    Joy! joy!
    For Alice has sworn to be mine!"

"Well! since, foolish boy, thou wilt never believe, —
  Nay, drain off that cup of red wine!
Then say who that bride is that comes from the church!
  Is it Alice who swore to be thine?
    Drink, boy!
    But Alice will never be thine!"

"Bring me a cup, — a brimming cup!
  Sparkling with rosy, red wine:
The blossoms of summer will bud, alas!
  But Alice will never be mine.
For women are gay, and light as the air,
  And faithless as faithless can be;
And their love is as fickle and false as the moon,
  As the winds, or the waves of the sea!"

HELEN.

SPLENDOR on her brow, —
 Beauty in her eye, —
Whiter than the snow,
 Bluer than the sky;
Shaped for rarest power,
 Gleaming with the light,
Beauty's richest dower,
 Beauty's sweetest might!
  Everything hath she
   That nature or that art
  Deemeth womanly,
   Save an honest heart!

On her cheek the rose
 Bloometh in its pride,
And the lily knows
 Where its rivals hide;
And the amorous South,
 Coming from the sea,
Knoweth not her mouth
 From the clover lea.
  Everything hath she
   That nature or that art
  Deemeth womanly,
   Save an honest heart!

Falling round her throat,
Marble white and bare,
In the soft winds float
Curls of sunny hair;
And her voice is clear
Like a bird's, and fills
Heart and soul and ear
With delicious thrills.
> *Everything hath she*
> *That nature or that art*
> *Deemeth womanly,*
> *Save an honest heart!*

Moveth she along
In her maiden prime,
Like a brilliant song
With a perfect rhyme;
Admiration bends
To her beauty, low:
There the homage ends —
For, alas! all know
> *Everything hath she*
> *That nature or that art*
> *Deemeth womanly,*
> *Save an honest heart.*

KNITTING.

She sits by the window, knitting, see!
  Her fingers small and white
Ply the shining needles, busily,
  From early morn till night;
    From early morn till night,
  Her fingers small and white
Ply the shining needles, busily,
  From early morn till night.

She sits by the window, knitting, see!
  How low she bends her head!
And over the needles, rapidly,
  Weaveth the colored thread;
    Weaveth the colored thread,
  As low she bends her head,
And over the needles, rapidly,
  Weaveth the colored thread.

She sits by the window, knitting, see!
  She works the glittering skein,
With her shining needles, curiously,
  That glance through the window pane;
    That glance through the window pane,
  As she works the glittering skein,
With her shining needles, curiously,
  That glance through the window pane.

She sits by the window, knitting, see!
  She holds it up to the light;
And her shining needles, cautiously,
  Pick the fallen stitch to her sight;
    Pick the fallen stitch to her sight,
  As she holds it up to the light,
Her shining needles, cautiously,
  Pick the fallen stitch to her sight.

She sits by the window, knitting, see!
  From morn to the evening's close;
And her shining needles, busily,
  Are weaving — what? who knows?
    Are weaving — what? who knows?
  From morn to the evening's close,
Her shining needles, busily,
  Are weaving — what? who knows?

THE MOSS ROSE.

The moss rose that she gave me,
    When we were both at school,
When she was like a singing-bird.
    And I a stupid fool;
The moss rose that she gave me, —
    Alas for me and her!
Too late I learned the language
    Of the little messenger.

The moss rose that she gave me
    I folded in my book;
And, years from then, I saw it all!
    The meaning and the look.
But, ah! the days had long gone by
    When we were both at school,
When she was like a singing-bird.
    And I a stupid fool.

The moss rose that she gave me,
    That in my book I thrust,
The stem is white and broken,
    And the leaves are blushing dust;
About my temples I can trace
    The glittering threads of snow;
And the singing-bird, from sorrow, flew
    To heaven, years ago.

GONE.

I.

Gone! gone at last, in brighter skies
    To his eternal rest!
Silent and still the blossom lies
    Upon its mother's breast;
Still folded to that faithful heart
As though, alas! they could not part.

II.

Though early with the morning sun
    They bore the child away,
And laid him where the waters run,
    And where the soft winds play;
And now the day his course fulfils
Behind the glowing western hills;

Yet there with tears and folded hands,
    And lips dumb with despair,
The mother by the cradle stands
    As though her boy were there;
His last dear bed with tears is wet —
She hath not strength to move it yet.

III.

We buried him beneath a tree
    Just down the meadow glade,
That, always, from the window, we
    Could see where he was laid;
And sometimes it seems hard to bear
The loss of one so young and fair.

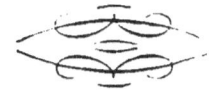

UP THE MOUNTAIN VALLEY.

Up the mountain valley,
  Hark, the rolling drum!
There our brethren rally,
  There the invaders come;
There our flag is waving,
  There a gallant band,
Foreign hirelings braving,
  For their country stand.

Hark! the charge is given!
  And their lines of steel
Freedom's band has riven,
  Like a thunder-peal;
On the horseman dashes!
  Down the hirelings go!
And the cannon flashes
  O'er a flying foe.

Up the mountain valley,
  In the setting sun,
There our brethren rally,
  And the fight is done;
Echoes through the gorges,
  As the invaders flee,
" Death to him who forges
  Fetters for the free!"

LOVE'S VAGARIES.

Little Love got mad one morning in May, —
'Twas one of his whimsical days, —
And he swore in his wrath, I am sorry to say,
    That the very old Nick he would raise!
So he mounted the back of a young butterfly
That he caught on the blow of a thistle just by,
And over his shoulder he slung in a trice
His bow with a quiver of arrows so nice;
And vowing to take, in the space of an hour,
Full vengeance on all who had scouted his power,
He threw his bare feet o'er the back of his steed,
And chirruped him off at the top of his speed.

Away, like the glance of the earliest dawn,
He rode on his yellow steed's wing;
His bow was all strained, and a keen arrow drawn,
    And set to the well-tightened string.
A Doctor, long famed for the cure of all ills,
Sat boxing his rarest and surest new pills,
And his rain-water drops and his ground rotten
    wood,
Ha, ha! said the Doctor, they're all just as good!
Twang went the bow! and the poor Doctor's face
Grew pale like a man's in a critical case;
Love left him preparing with cunningest art
A pill to relieve an attack of the heart.

Away, like the glance of the earliest dawn,
   Love rode on his yellow steed's wing.
His bow again strained, and a keen arrow drawn,
   And set to the well-tightened string.
A Lawyer well known for his quips and his cranks,
And the way he had played very fine legal pranks,
Was preparing a case just to come to the stand,
While the fees from both parties he held in his hand;
Twang went the bow! and the poor Lawyer's—la!
Looked as though in the case he'd discovered a flaw,
And the last of his practice that any one knew,
His suing and pleading, was pleading for Sue.

Away, like the glance of the earliest dawn,
   Love fled on his yellow steed's wing;
His bow again strained, and a fresh arrow drawn,
   And set to the well-tightened string.
A Clergyman who for some twenty years stood,
And preached to his flock as a clergyman should,
With fearful precision that moment had hurled
A bolt at the devil, the flesh, and the world;
Twang went the bow! 'tis reported when next
He preached to his flock he had taken the text,
And had by authority perfectly shown
That for man 'twas not good that he should be alone.

Away, like the glance of the earliest dawn,
    Love fled on his yellow steed's wing,
His bow again strained, and a fresh arrow drawn,
    And set to the well-tightened string.
An Editor sat in his sanctum up stairs,
Directing the ways of all human affairs,
And stealing "original" quietly out
From a pile of exchanges he'd scattered about;
Twang went the bow! but the editor's eye
Never turned, for he thought 'twas the bite of a fly!
The arrow that bounded away from his side
Like pigeon-shot from the rhinoceros' hide,
On the exchange he was cutting unluckily flew,
And his rusty old scissors just snipped it in two!

N'IMPORTE.

She loved me when my father held
    Bank stock and cash and cattle,
When to her door my splendid grays
    At five o'clock would rattle;
Ah! how, in some romantic spot
    As rolled the cushioned carriage,
She blushed and sighed at all my talk
    Of wedded love and marriage!

At all the routs and all the balls
    I was her constant suitor;
And Tom and Ned stood back, because
    They knew I had the pewter;
And though Miss Brown and Mrs. Smith,
    'Twas said, felt rather nettled,
Yet all the gossips in the town
    Declared the thing was settled.

So shone the sun, until one day
    My father's name was doubted! —
She only sighed and wept at first,
    And bit her lip and pouted;
But when the bank went down, the sky
    Portended stormy weather,
And next day week the stocks and I
    Went down the tide together!

I swore from twelve to one o'clock,
    At two was hardly righted,
And up to three I felt, 'tis true,
    A very little slighted.
'Twas very hard for one so young
    To read the truth in minion,
That gold is the specific part
    Of Love's resplendent pinion.

No matter! — let it pass — 'tis true
    I loved with boyish passion,
And trimmed my hair and wore my coat
    Exactly in the fashion;
Some little pains I took to please
    Her sister and her mother,
Discussed her father's Saxonies,
    Drank soda with her brother.

I wrote some letters which were warm,
    Some sonnets which were tender,
And gilt-edged notes and *billet-doux*
    By reams I used to send her;
I went to church, if she was there!
    Three times a day on Sunday;
And asked her mother how she liked
    The sermon, every Monday.

It cost me something for the "Gems"
    And "Tokens" that I bought her,
And something at the jeweller's
    For rings and orange water;

And in my bill at Brown's I found
  An item rather thrifty. —
" To horse and chaise, at sundry times,"
  Some forty dollars, fifty.

Well — I have lived to bless the good
  My early lesson taught me,
To quietly enjoy the fruits
  That time and luck have brought me ;
A busy hand has filled my purse
  With many a golden clinker ;
And she, I hear, on Ripton Flats
  Is stopping with a tinker !

A CHANGE.

She glided down the mazy dance,
   All eyes upon her glancing,
And everybody vowed, who saw,
   'Twas floating more than dancing;
The bluest eye, the rosiest cheek,
   A lip like morning weather
When on the flower and grass you have
   The dew and sun together.

The beaux, half crazy, seemed intent
   Upon their own destruction,
And crowding round her where she sat,
   Begged for an introduction;
And everybody sought her hand,
   And everybody wondered
If she were worth a thousand, or
   Were worth a cool five hundred.

Again she glided down the dance,
   A single season after,
And there was still as much of fun,
   Of music, mirth, and laughter;
Her cheek was still as fair and sweet,
   Her lip as soft and rosy,
But yet about her charms the beaux
   Had grown most strangely prosy!

A fellow in a white cravat,
  And vest of latest trimming,
Through waltz with her and through quadrille
  Familiarly was swimming.
And when the dance was done, I saw
  Her fan and salts he carried;
And then the thing was clear enough, —
  Alas! the girl was married!

ELLEN VAN DUZEE.

Miss Ellen was a pretty girl,
 As every body knew;
She wore a satin-beaver hat,
 A very little shoe.
Her lips were like the berry of —
 You've seen the mountain ash?
Her figure, like the cedar. She'd
 Considerable cash.

She'd worshippers from far and near,
 Some fifty in them all,
And partners by the million at
 The last Thanksgiving ball;
And many a fop looked mellow things,
 And many a dandy sad,
While fortune-hunters, as they snapped
 Their fingers, cried, "Egad!"

Oh! many an offer Ellen had,
 And many a vow had she,
She soon became so sorely pressed,
 'Twas very sad to see;
But all her offers, somehow 'twas,
 She didn't like them much —
She looked upon love's agony
 As 'twere the blankest Dutch.

They thronged her parties, ate her cake,
  And drank her father's wine;
They talked of broken hearts and sighed —
  To her 'twas all moonshine.
She never seemed to care a straw
  About their sighs and tears;
That they were getting into debt,
  And she somewhat in years.

One April day there came to town
  — It was the twenty-fourth —
A Southern chap who seemed to be
  On business at the North.
He purposed, so 'twas said, to stop
  Until the last of May;
But June came round, and his affairs
  Required still further stay.

'Twas rather strange, the people thought —
  What could his business be?
But soon conjecture ended with —
  " He's rich and twenty-three!"
He saw Miss Ellen, it was true;
  Danced with her at a ball;
And said some pretty things, of course:
  But this, it seemed, was all.

And so affairs went on, and he
  Was welcomed everywhere:
The older ladies liked his cash,
  The younger liked his hair!

At last a story got afloat,
    And like a wild-fire flew,
That Polly Peep had said she knew
    Exactly *what* she knew!

Ah! there was strange commotion then
    Among fair Ellen's beaux!
And there was one — his name was Smith;
    John Smith, you may suppose —
Who talked particularly large
    Beneath his little hat,
And swore upon his honor he
    Would put a stop to that!

He said he'd been to New Orleans,
    And owned a Spanish dirk,
Had fought ten duels, winged, at times,
    Three Russians and a Turk;
He hinted to the stranger that
    The world was rather round!
And asked him if he'd ever seen
    The general burying-ground!

But time and tide will never wait,
    Our old grandmothers say;
And both about this time went on
    Their old accustomed way.
September came and went, and still
    The stranger was in town,
And it was thought when Smith looked up
    He looked a little down.

One Sabba' day, just after " Old
    Mortality" was sung,
While yet upon the parson's lips
    The benediction hung,
Lo! suddenly the old Town Clerk,
    That venerable man!
Ahemed three times, and then, at length,
    With lifted voice began: —

" I take this opportunity
    To publish in this place,
That marriage is intended 'tween,
    By God's permitting grace,
John Hamilton McNeal, Esquire,
    Of Western Tennessee,
And"— silence hushed its breath to hear—
    " And Ellen Van Duzee!"

Then came the scowl and smothered curse,
    Hints of percussion locks,
As Smith rose up, and — shut the lid
    Of his tobacco-box!
At first, to heal his sorrows, he'd
    Attach her father's lands!
And then he winked, and felt relieved
    To have her off his hands!

At last he thought that, after all,
    'Twas not so great a catch,
And rather pitied Mac because
    He'd made so bad a match!

He knew some things, he thought he did! —
Could make disclosures which —
Old Van Duzee — notes — borrowed cash —
Not everlasting rich!

The wedding came, and Ellen's beaux
  Were welcomed to the scene;
And most of them got dreadful blue
  Because they'd been so green!
Next morning Ellen started off
  To Nashville on her way,
And left some folks to think of things
  They're thinking of this day.

COUNT SWAGERDORFF.

Miss Emily Angeline Agatha Jane
   Clementina Victoria Sleeper
Fell in love with the elegant Count Swagerdorff,
   A foreigner just from the Dnieper.
He had cash by the ocean, the people all said;
   And yet, I persist in it stoutly,
That never occurred to Miss Agatha's 'ma
   When she smiled on the Count so devoutly!

Count Swagerdorff's whiskers were large, and so
   black!
And his hair lay in *such* pretty ringlets!
Who could wonder that love, who is blind as they
   say,
   Found the curls tangled up with his winglets?
Count Swagerdorff's eyes — ah, how soft and how
   blue!
And his voice was like zephyrs that mingle
Their murmurs at eve on the bosom of June —
   He wore on his finger a single

Gold ring with a stone of remarkable cost;
   His waist was as small as a lady's,
And his cheek and his lip were as red and as
   warm
   As they say are the young girls of Cadiz.

His feet and his hands were of noble-blood size,
    And he trod the old earth with such *hauteur*
No wonder Miss Agatha's suitors all fled
    In despair, when Count Swagerdorff sought her.

Count Swagerdorff danced, and Count Swager-
    dorff sung,
    Count Swagerdorff played very finely,
Spoke Russian and Spanish, Italian and French,
    And lolled on a sofa divinely.
In English he'd learned a thousand sweet songs,
    Whose virtue some think rather brittle;
Could repeat Parisina, Don Juan, and all
    Of Tom Moore in his *sobriquet*, Little.

Count Swagerdorff spoke to Miss Agatha's 'pa,
    And declared his affections were blighted,
Unless the sweet hand of his daughter were his,—
    Miss Agatha's 'pa was delighted!
So the thing was all settled at once, and the day!
Ere June a May blossom had wilted,
The day was appointed. The cake and the dress
    Were done, and the comforter quilted.

Count Swagerdorff sat at his hotel at tea
    With a *noli me tangere* phiz on.
When the sheriff came in, in search of a chap
    Who had broke from the Windsor State Prison.
Count Swagerdorff laughed, and Count Swager-
    dorff frowned;
    But the fellow grew saucy and bolder,

Walked up to his chair with, "How are ye, my
  bird!"
  And laid a broad hand on his shoulder.

Count Swagerdorff looked at the man with a stare,
  And called on the landlord to take him
Away; then ordered his servant, black Sam,
  To collar the scoundrel and shake him.
But the fellow just gave Count Swagerdorff's curls
  A brush with his hands in the scuffle;
And, alas! 'twas all up with Jim Brown, and his
  wrists
  Were quietly graced with a ruffle.

So they marched Count Swagerdorff back to his
  cell,
  With a face on that could not be painted;
Poor Agatha's 'pa and Agatha's 'ma! —
  One swore, and the other she fainted.
And the laugh of the town was the source of
  great pain,
  When the Count left the place with his keeper,
To — ladies, the moral I pray you will heed —
  Miss Angeline Agatha Sleeper.

KATE WAS ONCE A LITTLE GIRL.

Kate was once a little girl,
    Heigh-ho! heigh-ho!
Eyes of blue and teeth of pearl,
    Heigh-ho! heigh-ho!
In the spring when school was done,
Full of life and full of fun,
O'er the hills away she'd run,
    Heigh-ho! heigh-ho!

Gentle breezes all the day,
    Heigh-ho! heigh-ho!
Through her sunny locks would play,
    Heigh-ho! heigh-ho!
All her thoughts were pure and bright
As the stars we see at night,
Shining with a joyous light,
    Heigh-ho! heigh-ho!

Kate's a little older now,
    Heigh-ho! heigh-ho!
Still as fair her radiant brow,
    Heigh-ho! heigh-ho!
Still on her cheek as brightly plays
The sunshine of her youthful days,
And still as sweet her girlish ways,
    Heigh-ho! heigh-ho!

Care may scowl and age may blame,
    Heigh-ho! heigh-ho!
Kate will always be the same,
    Heigh-ho! heigh-ho!
        tly Time shall steal away,
            be as bright and gay
              laughed in girlhood's day,
            igh-ho! heigh-ho!

THE YELLOW CORN.

Come, boys, sing! —
Sing of the yellow corn;
Sing, boys, sing,
Sing of the yellow corn!
He springeth up from the fallow soil,
With the blade so green and tall;
And he payeth well the reaper's toil,
When the husks in the autumn fall.
The pointed leaves,
And the golden ear,
The rustling sheaves,
In the ripened year —
Sing, boys, sing!
Sing of the yellow corn;
Sing, boys, sing,
Sing of the yellow corn.

He drinks the rain in the summer long
And he loves the streams that run,
And he sends the stalk so stout and strong,
To bask in the summer sun.
The pointed leaves,
And the golden ear,
The rustling sheaves,
In the ripened year —
Sing, boys, sing!
Sing of the yellow corn;
Sing, boys, sing,
Sing of the yellow corn.

He loves the dews of the starry night,
And the breathing wind that plays
With his tassels green, when the mellow light
Of the moon on the meadow stays.
  The pointed leaves,
   And the golden ear,
  The rustling sheaves,
   In the ripened year —
    Sing, boys, sing!
     Sing of the yellow corn;
    Sing, boys, sing,
     Sing of the yellow corn.

A glorious thing is the yellow corn.
With the blade so green and tall;
A blessed thing is the yellow corn,
When the husks in the autumn fall.
  Then, sing, boys, sing!
   Sing of the yellow corn;
  Sing, boys, sing,
   Sing of the yellow corn.
  The pointed leaves,
   And the golden ear,
  The rustling sheaves,
   In the ripened year —
    Come, sing, boys, sing,
     Sing of the yellow corn;
    Sing, boys, sing,
     Sing of the yellow corn!

TO LILY.

PRETTY Lily, dearest Lily,
  Pray what shall I do
With my head so full of verses,
  My heart so full of you?

All my time and all my sonnets,
  All my thoughts, you claim;
I am nothing, dearest Lily,
  Nothing but a name.

I am nothing, dearest Lily,
  E'en myself I miss;
Lily, Lily, wicked Lily,
  You're to blame for this.

Pretty Lily, dearest Lily,
  Pray what *shall* I do
With my head so full of verses,
  And my heart of you?

THE HOMESTEAD.

'Tis many a day since in the spring,
    My own sweet native dell,
I bade thee, with a sad, sad heart,
    My first and long farewell;
'Tis many a day, — yes, many a year, —
    And yet, as then, I see
My mother waving, from the door,
    A long good-bye to me.

My dearest mother! Sad and strange
    Has been the lot I've known
Since when that morn thy loving arms
    About my neck were thrown;
And scarcely now remains a line
    My boyish features wore
When looked I last on home, — to me
    A home, alas! no more.

Of those I left, long years ago,
    Around that old hearth-stone,
Two perished when the leaves grew pale
    Beneath the autumn sun;
And those who still remain of all
    That gay and thoughtless band,
Changed, like the place that gave them birth,
    Are scattered o'er the land.

Still onward sweeps the tide that bears
  Us to our long, dark home ;
And, whereso'er our lot be cast.
  Together we shall come,
And lay our heads upon the lap
  Of our good mother ; there
Shall sleep and peace be ours once more,
  And rest from toil and care.

SWEET ALICE GRAY.

WOULD that I had loved thee never,
    Sweet Alice Gray;
Then thine image would not ever
    Haunt me by day;

And this struggle to forget thee,
    Sweet Alice Gray,
Had not worn, if I'd not met thee,
    My life away.

Grew my love to thee as groweth,
    Sweet Alice Gray,
Where alone the wild brook floweth,
    Flowers by the way.

Still I hoped till hope was banished,
    Sweet Alice Gray,
And my star of life has vanished
    Ever away.

THE WORLD GOES ROUND AND ROUND.

The world goes round and round, they say;
    They say that the world goes round;
'Twas lucky, no doubt, that by some great man
    This very great truth was found!
For how should we know that the world goes round,
    That the world goes round and round;
Unless it had been, that, by some great man,
    This very great truth had been found?

There are other strange things, as I have been told,
    Besides that the world goes round;
And others as strange, I'm inclined to think,
    That nobody yet has found;
But still it is certain, about the world,
    That the world goes round and round;
And that by some great man, sometime in the world,
    This very great truth has been found.

Well! since it is true that the world goes round,
    That the world goes round and round;
That we stand on our feet, on our feet, you see!
    While the world goes round and round;
Why, then let the world *go* round and round,
    Let the world go round and be shot!
I suspect it is bound to go round and round,
    Whether *you* and *I* like it or not!

SONG.

Is she coy and is she wary,
    Flying from your suit;
Do her lips and passions vary,
    Like her idle lute?

Vex the girl with frozen glances,
    Taunt her with your eye,
Woo another with advances;
    From *her* presence fly!

Soon the heart will change the fashion
    Of the tongue's deceit;
Lips no more deny the passion;
    Eyes no longer cheat.

THE POET.

He was dying in his garret,
   And his cheek was thin and white ;
But his soul was full of music,
   And his eye was full of light.
He saw a radiant Vision,
   And its awful presence smote
His sickly blood to fever,
   And he seized his pen and wrote.

He wrote — Into his window
   The light of morning streamed,
And the poet from his labor
   Looked up as one who dreamed :
He saw the early sunshine
   Glance round his restless pen ;
But the Vision still was with him,
   And he saw and wrote again.

He wrote — Into his window
   The setting sunlight streamed,
And the poet from his labor
   Awoke as one who dreamed :
He saw the fading shadows
   Grow dark upon his floor ;
The Vision had departed,
   And he saw and wrote no more.

And never in his garret
  Was the poet seen again :
His humble name had faded
  From the memory of men.
His hand and brain had failed him,
  Though his heart was stout and strong ;
And he died, alone, but trusting
  To the glory of his song.

From the hovel to the palace
  A mighty sound is heard,
And the nations seem to ponder
  O'er a bright and glorious Word ;
And armies rush to battle,
  And the millions, in their might,
Dash down their chains forever,
  In their battling for the right !

'Twas the Vision of the Poet !
  'Twas the Word he wrote, at last,
That thrilled through all the millions
  Like a fearful trumpet blast ;
'Twas the Vision of the Poet !
  'Twas the Song he wrote ! — 'Twas done
The armies sang his battle-songs,
  And victories were won !

O ye who labor, doubting,
  Growing sullen at the wrong ;
When few seem to be listening
  To the music of your song !

Write! write in faith, and upward
    Let your glance be on the sky:
The Prophets never perish;
    True singers never die.

RETALIATION.

"Well! here they are, — the letters which
  You sent me years ago;
They're somewhat soiled, as you will see, —
  Of course they'd be, you know.
I need not say what they contain,
  Perhaps it is not meet;
Nor what you told me, will I take
  The trouble to repeat."

"What *did* I say, that now I have
  The honor of a call,
From one I scarcely recollect,
  And never knew at all?"
"No matter now: we will not have
  A single word of strife;
I understood you, though, to say
  This spring you'd be my wife."

"Perhaps I did; but I was young,
  And now have quite forgot
That silly freak of childish love,
  And wonder you have not;
Besides, I'm sure, whate'er I said,
  I never did intend
To seem to you more than I was, —
  Your most devoted friend."

" All just as well : good morning, ma'am !
    Oh ! do you know, they say
That Colonel Charles Fitz Albert Hill
    Last evening ran away ;
Intending to return, no doubt,
    Ned Hunter's watch and chain ? —
I see the papers state, besides,
    He has a wife in Maine."

" Impossible ! how could the man !
    The wretch ! deceive me so ?
'Tis dreadful ! Oh ! how can I bear,
    How can I bear this blow ? "
" Good morning, ma'am ! I hope you'll feel " —
    " Forgive me ! on my life
I've loved you only — didn't you say
    That I should be your wife ? "

" Perhaps I did ; but I was young,
    And now have quite forgot
That silly freak of childish love,
    And wonder you have not !
Besides, I'm sure, whate'er I said,
    I never did intend
To seem to you more than I was, —
    Your most devoted friend."

I STOOD BESIDE THE SEA.

I STOOD beside the sea, —
　　The billows, soft and slow
Came drifting up the sands to me,
　　Like wreaths of winter snow;
And she, who smiled upon the shore,
　　Her soft hand clasped in mine,
Thought not of those who dream no more
　　Beneath the cruel brine.

I stood beside the sea, —
　　The ship had left the land,
And, waving sad farewell to me,
　　She kissed and kissed her hand;
I prayed the sea be true and fair, —
　　Alas! the treacherous tide,
Enamoured of her golden hair,
　　Despoiled me of my bride.

I stand beside the sea, —
　　I curse the faithless tide,
I curse the false and craven sea,
　　That robbed me of my bride!
It moans and writhes, like one who yearns
　　A damning sin to flee;
But never more my bride returns,
　　Ah! — never more to me!

PART II.

HYMN.

(Written for the occasion of the dedication of GREEN-MOUNT
CEMETERY, at Montpelier, Vt., Sept. 15, 1855.)

This fairest spot of hill and glade,
   Where blooms the flower and waves the tree,
And silver streams delight the shade,
   We consecrate, O Death! to thee.

Here all the months the year may know
   Shall watch this " Eden of the Dead,"
To wreathe with flowers, or crown with snow,
   The dreamless sleeper's narrow bed.

And when above its graves we kneel,
   Resigning to the mouldering urn
The friends whose silent hearts shall feel
   No balmy summer's glad return,

Each marble shaft our hands may rear,
   To mark where dust to dust is given,
Shall lift its chiselled column here
   To point our tearful eyes to heaven.

A HYMN.

(A Fragment.)

Praise ye the Lord of hill and dell!
　Praise ye the Lord of earth and sky!
Praise ye the Lord! Let the anthem swell
　To Judah's God on high.

He sends the rain on thirsty hills;
His bounty Labor's basket fills;
And the flowers that live by the water's brim
With their scented breath acknowledge him.

Then, praise ye the Lord of hill and dell!
　Praise ye the Lord of earth and sky!
Praise ye the Lord! Let the glad song swell
　To Judah's God on high.

AN EVENING IN SUMMER.

(A Fragment.)

The sun is down ; dark grow the glades ;
  The stars are gathering in the deep ;
And, o'er the earth, night's misty shades
  Are stealing like a quiet sleep.
The wild winds, wandering through the sky,
  Stoop from their paths as day declines,
And nestle, with a shivering cry
  And weary wing, among the pines.

I'LL TUNE MY HARP TO DREAMS NO MORE.

I'LL tune my harp to dreams no more,
  No more to idle song;
'Tis time to strike to war and strife, —
  To war against the Wrong.
While Might still holds his throttling grasp
  On Freedom's blackened throat,
And o'er the earth the robber-flags
  Of red Oppression float;

While tongues are stifled, Right borne down,
  And Error's banded host
In triumph tramples down the Truth
  With coarse and mocking boast;
While, scowling, still sits brutal Force
  In sweet Persuasion's place,
And low Lust turns his serpent-eye
  On shrinking Virtue's face;

While Luxury shuts her marble halls
  On Hunger, wild and gaunt;
While some in swollen surfeit live,
  And millions die of want: —
I'll tune my harp to dreams no more,
  No more to idle song;
I'll strike its chords for war and strife, —
  For war against the Wrong!

REQUIESCAT.

'Tis finished, and Death's sleep at last
  Has settled on thy pallid brow;
And anguish, strife, and pain have passed,
  And left thee to thy slumbers now;
As steals the mother from her child
  By soft and quiet slumbers blest,
So passed thy soul, when sleep had wiled
  Thy weary body into rest.

So quiet is thy marble face,
  So few the marks of strife appear,
That scarce a line is left to trace
  That Death has done his mission here.
Fair through thy lids the blue veins shine;
  Thy cheek is hardly paler; while,
Life-like around those lips of thine,
  Is lingering still a gentle smile.

Thou'rt only sleeping!—round thy bed
  Thy children gather as before;
And bend above thy shrouded head,
  And ask to kiss thy lips once more.
Thou'rt only sleeping!—speak to us!
  In vain! Thy eyes are closed and dark.
In vain we weep and call thee thus;—
  Gone is the bright ethereal spark.

Forever gone! and yet there's left
  No trace behind, no clew to tell
Where it hath wandered; cold, bereft,
  The form we loved so long and well
Lies motionless. The life that yearned
  For freedom from the sickly clay,
Escaped at last from Death, has turned
  From sorrow to the cloudless day.

The song of birds, the fitful breeze,
  Henceforth to thee are nothing. Near
Thy dwelling winds shall stir the trees;
  But nothing to thy drowsy ear
Shall be the thunder, or the tread
  Above thee. Gentle summer rains
Shall prattle o'er thy narrow bed;
  And, clothed in beauty, all the plains

Shall yellow with the yellowing corn:
  But thou shalt know the harvest moon,
The increase of the autumn morn,
  The darkness of the winter noon,
No more. For thee the flowers shall keep
  Their sweets in vain; the shouting floods
Awaken; and the warm winds sweep
  To music all the budding woods.

A time, and those thy life has nursed
  Can claim no kindred to thee there;
From thy short being still shall burst
  New life, and many a form shall bear,

Unconsciously, thine image, when
   Thy name has perished, or will seem,
Far down the race of by-gone men,
   A dim and half-remembered dream.

Yet, passing from us, thou dost leave
   The never-failing trust to those
Who, summoned round thy pillow, grieve,
   That from thy dull and void repose
Thou all renewed shalt rise and take,
   Where life is ever blossoming,
A form more beautiful, and wake
   From darkness to perpetual spring.

Farewell! we wrap thee in thy shroud,
   And bear thee to thy long-sought rest:
So hushed, it seems a breath aloud
   Would jar to life thy pulseless breast.
Sleep! envying thee, we rather mourn
   Our lot to weep and suffer here,
To feel each day some new tie torn,
   And see some loved one disappear.

THE MOTHERLESS.

(FRAGMENT.)

Sweet child! she's weary with her play;
  And o'er her, like the spell
Of music at the close of day,
  Sleep stealeth. Arabel!
I gaze upon thee and I bless
Thee, beautiful and motherless.

Thankful to Heaven that thou art thus
  Upon our bounty thrown;
Thou'rt welcome! share our lot with us,
  As though thou wert our own;
All thou has lost we'll seek to be,
Through all thy life, sweet child, to thee.

I see she cometh from the hills!
  And in her bosom presses
The flowers she gathers from the rills.
  Lilies and water-cresses;
Yet none of all are half so fair
As she with her soft Saxon hair.

Well may these flowers, so sweet and pure,
  Shrink from her breast away:
They cannot, envious things, endure
  A flower more fair than they;
If all that envy her came here,
The fields were rather bare, I fear.

BOY LOVE.

Years, years ago, when life was new,
    A wild and laughing girl
Lived up the lane, with eyes of blue,
    And many a golden curl.
Forever hand in hand we ran,—
    Two beings with one life;
Ah! how I wished I were a man
    To " wed my little wife"!

She sleeps upon a grassy hill,
    Where, in the autumn night,
Upon the elm the whip-poor-will
    Sings in the pale moon-light.
The stone we raised above her head
    Is broken and defaced;
The sunken earth above her bed
    Shows where the child was placed.

I pass along the road at night,
    And, leaning on the stile,
Think of her face, all love and light,
    Her bright and sunny smile;
And o'er my heart my childish grief,
    That sad and early dream,
Steals, like the shadow of a leaf
    Along a summer stream.

A FRAGMENT.

"And that!"
              " That was a charger's neigh,
When they harness him for a battle day,
And the rider strives to check him in vain
With a goad of the spur and a jerk of the rein:
And there comes a sound, this way to the right,
Like forming men for a coming fight; —
Does the sentry hear it?"
              " Yes!
              Through the street,
There's a sudden sound of trampling feet,
And, — ho! that glare o'er the city's gloom!
  Up to the sky how that rocket sings!
While, starting up from his dreams of home,
  Each Briton on the rampart springs."

" The plain grows dark as the moon goes down,
And shadows huge o'er the city frown,
Like wrathful giants; over the wall
The flags of the tyrant rise and fall,
The — "
      " Hark! what was that? there, — that! did
              you hear?"
" No! what was it? where was it? near?"
" And that?"

"Was the wail of a bugle" —
"No!
'Twas more like the wind when its breath is low —"
"There! that! what was that?"
"That was the blast, —
No, 'twas a horseman riding fast."

. . . .

THE AMERICAN.

HALF covered by the wild woodbine
And scented by the brake,
O'ershadowed by the princely pine,
And mirrowed in the lake ;
Oh! dearer far to him than all
The pomp of foreign lands,
The humble cot his labor builds
With free, unshackled hands.

He gazes on his mother-land,
Her rivers rolling by,
Her monarch mountains, as they stand,
Their blue peaks in the sky,
To brave the fury of the storms
That round their heads have birth ;

Her plains, where life in all its forms
Wakes from the nursing earth, —
And asks himself, with manly pride,
Where is the land like this,
Of mountain, flood, and prairie wide,
And solemn wilderness?

While others boast of lordly hall,
Of regal pomp and pride,
Of fallen mosque and mouldering wall,
And fields where kings have died ;

Of crumbling tombs and monuments.
  Round which, when time was young,
The wandering Arabs pitched their tents
  And wild war chants were sung;

Of banners brave, and flags that love
  To look on riven shields,
Whose haughty folds have waved above
  A thousand battle-fields;
Of Bannockburn, Pultowa's day,
  Napoleon's bloody star,
Of Marathon, Thermopylæ,
  Of Bosworth, Trafalgar, —

He treads the land of Bunker Hill!
  Where Yorktown's day was won,
Where looks upon Potomac still
  The tomb of Washington;
And boasts of sacred battle-plains,
  Where, by oppression driven,
A nation broke a tyrant's chains
  With blows for freedom given.

MY UNCLE JERRY.

I.

Just round the corner, up the street,
    Among the elms and maples,
Beyond the noise of trucks and cars
    And rush of Northern staples;
Where ladies never promenade
    To show their latest dresses,
And where the loud, uneasy tide
    Of business never presses,—

There stands a mansion, built before
    You ever saw a steeple,
Ere Treasury notes and Tariff acts
    Had vexed a growing people;
When the Hampshire Grants were tracts of land
    Somewhat in disputation,
Tracked by the most untractable
    Of all the Yankee nation;

When Ethan Allen ruled the State
    With steel and stolen scriptur',
Declared his "beech-seal" war against
    New York, and took and whipt her:
A gambrel-roofed, one-story house,
    In front a tall black cherry;
And there, a type of olden times,
    Resides my uncle Jerry.

II.

A noble, old-school gentleman,
    A personage quite rare
In these exquisite modern times
    Of stays, rattans, and hair:
One of your true, world-hearted men,
    Whose purse and store and basket
Are always open, and whose heart
    Is yours before you ask it.

Prompt, courteous, and dignified,
    With few but meaning words;
He never plays at mediums;
    He knows no halves or thirds:
And never, like some Yankees, stops
    To reckon, s'pose, or guess;
But everything goes with a *ve-*
    Ni vidi vici-ness.

A very temperate man is he,
    Though it is true, no doubt,
He had his "train," when, years ago,
    The "Flood-wood" was called out;
And though of "Rum" not very shy,
    Yet little of a rover,
He wisely chose to be on land
    When he was "half-seas over."

So honest, too, that through a life
    Of sharp and constant dealing,
He never took a cent or dime
    But with the kindest feeling.

And never made a charge that he
  In conscience thought was skittish;
Not e'en the charge, 'tis said, he made
  At Plattsburgh, on the British.

He wears a rather longish cue
  Tied with a ribbon black,
That hangs itself most solemnly
  Adown my uncle's back.
His snuff-box is a relic of
  The days of old Queen Ann;
A Dutchman's name is on the lid,
  'Tis—something after Van.

My uncle still adheres to shoes
  With buckles on the top,
And still about his dress you see
  He might have been a fop!
When he was young and in his prime,
  And frolics were in vogue,
I've heard some ancient spinsters say
  He was a " wicked rogue ! "

And even now, when he recounts
  His days of youth and glory,
He'll make my aunt look daggers with
  Some rather rakish story:—
You'd laugh to see him cock his eye.
  As by the light-stand sitting,
She seems intent to find the stitch
  She'd just dropped in her knitting!

His hickory cane, you always see
    He carries in his hand,
With smooth-worn knots and loosened point,
    And polished golden band;
Where, half effaced, his name is carved
    Upon the ivory head,—
He brought from old Connecticut,
    As I have heard it said.

With children never blest, he frets
    And scolds at neighbor Pickens;
And wonders why he need to let
    His act so like "the dickens."
If *he* had children, if he *had*,
    By old John Jacob Astor!—
(He always swears by him) — he'd see —
    He'd see who'd be the master.

III.

He talks of politics sometimes;
    Although he never spends
Much time or sense, in latter years,
    Disputing with his friends.
Though somewhat pugilistic once,
    And famous in a row,
The men he fought, he says, are dead,—
    Sha'n't fight their children now!

But if you'd know what times we had
    With John Munro and Tryon;
The mighty stir they made about
    The people's Matthew Lyon;

Or anything of matters, when
    Our freedom we were winning,—
He'll talk from dark to twelve o'clock,
    And that for a beginning.

He'll tell you how, in '83,
    To Guilford Allen went,
To quell in that Republic, there,
    Some little discontent;
The time, you know, the Colonel swore,
    And looked upon their farms,
He'd Sodom-and-Gomorrah 'em.
    If they didn't stack their arms!

And how the Yorker part stood out,
    And swung their scythes and axes,
And swore by all 'twas black and white
    They wouldn't pay their taxes;
How Bradley left the town without
    A Lamb among her birches,
And Mrs. Hunt's ungodly son
    Despoiled her of her Churches.

How John Munro came on, one day,
    With all his Yorker train,
And took Remember Baker up,
    And — set him down again.
How one Ben Hough, who practised law
    And freedom in his speech,
Received in full for services
    A fine back-load of beech.

He'll tell you how for years we lived
    Without a constitution,
And put the laws we made, in force
    With perfect execution ;
When the Prophets and Committees were
    Our only Legislators,
And Seth and Ethan, of the law,
    The sole administrators.

IV.

There's much, he says, about Vermont
    For history and song ;
Much to be written yet, and much
    That has been written wrong.
The Old Thirteen, united, fought
    The Revolution through ;
While, single-handed, old Vermont
    Fought them, and England, too.

She'd Massachusetts and New York,
    And — so the record stands —
New Hampshire, England, Guilford, and
    The Union on her hands ;
Yet still her Single Star above
    Her hills triumphant shone,
And when the smoke of battle passed —
    She'd whipt them all, alone !

Talk, says my uncle, growing warm,
    About the South and West !
Far's I know, they are well enough,
    Their lands may be the best :

But when you come talk of men,
    You may depend upon't,
No State can boast of such a race
    Of people, as Vermont.

They, independent as the winds
    That fanned them where they stood ;
They were the men who took old Ti',
    Because they thought they would !
They were the men, who, through Champlain,
    Swept on to Montreal ;
The first to strike, the last to yield,
    At Freedom's battle-call.

Insulted by neglect, — when they
    For simple justice called,
With contumely turned away,
    By rank oppression galled,—
They were the men to stand alone,
    Alone their rights maintain,
Alone their battles fight and win,
    Alone their freedom gain.

And when the record shall be made,
    And their position shown,
Their struggles clearly understood,
    Their conquests fairly known, —
No men of any clime or age
    In history will outshine
The heroes of the Single Star,
    The Doe's-head and the Pine.

The Allens, Thomas Chittenden,
   And Bradley (Stephen Roe),
Paul Spooner, Baker, Haswell, Hunt,
   And many more, you know;
Seth Warner, Fassett, Tichenor,
   The Robinsons and Fays, —
Are men. my uncle thinks, to grace
   A nation's proudest days.

V.

But I can never tell you half —
   You'd better call and see
My uncle with his solemn cue,
   And buckles on his knee;
He'll entertain you many an hour
   With things 'twere vain to write,
And keep you listening to his talk,
   And laughing, half the night.

You'll find a welcome in the style
   Our fathers ate and drank;
A welcome free and full to all,
   With little care for rank;
The style that by the table showed
   A bountiful provider,
When the parson blessed the food prepared,—
   And took his mug of cider.

VI.

But uncle Jerry's getting old,
   And leans upon his cane;

He tries to walk erect, but then,
    It gives my uncle pain ;
My cousin Ellen ties his cue,
    And reads the latest papers,
And sings his favorite songs when he
    Seems troubled with the vapors.

Poor fellow, he will soon be done !
    He never liked a bank, —
The chains of death are riveting,
    'Tis sad to hear them clank :
I'm sorry — I shall miss his " hem ! "
    And his accustomed " Jerry !
I say, my boy, you'll go it yet ;
    You're like your' uncle, very ! "

OLD MARGARET.

I.

There is a poor old woman
  Lives down below the mill,
Just where the turnpike-road begins
  To struggle up the hill.

Below the mill this woman lives,
  Below the mill, alone;
A very strange old woman.
  The strangest ever known.

Some fifty years ago her hut
  Of logs was built, they say;
And since they made the river road
  'Tis almost in the way.

So when you rattle down the hill,
  If you're in reckless mood,
Be careful, or your wheel will hit
  Her scanty pile of wood;

A little heap of mouldy bark,
  And strips of boards and sticks,
That from the river's neighb'ring brink
  In heavy rains she picks.

A little brook that, 'cross the road,
  Creeps through the gray stone-wall,
And to the river, just below,
  Glides with an easy fall,

With purest water through the year,
  And never known to fail,
Fills from a rude and mossy spout
  Old Margaret's water-pail.

And those, and they are very few,
  Her fancy deigns to heed,
Supply her small necessities
  With all she seems to need.

And so this poor old woman
  Lives down below the mill.
Just where the turnpike road begins
  To struggle up the hill.

This very poor old woman
Below the mill, alone,
This very strange old woman,
The strangest ever known.

Sometimes, for hours, beside the brook,
  In summer she will stand,
Her gray locks straggling round her neck,
  A willow in her hand,

And scold and blame the little stream
   That ripples in the sun,
Because so very swift to her
   Its current seems to run.

And then, a moment gazing down
   Its soft and quiet flow,
She stoops, with sharp and angry words
   And quick and fretful blow;

And strikes her stick across its face,
   Intent with flashing eyes,
And stamping fiercely, " Faster, now!"
   And " Faster still!" she cries.

Within her hut, so poor and old,
   So desolate and mean,
Besides herself, no living thing,
   'Tis said, is ever seen;

Except, that in a marble vase,
   Carved by the subtlest art
To represent a maiden's hand
   Clasped round a broken heart.

A strange and nameless plant, at times,
   Is seen upon the floor,
Its curious colors shaded and
   Half hidden by the door;

And this she seems to watch and nurse
With never-ending care,
And, when it blossoms, from her vase
Finds little time to spare.

Whence came the plant, or what its name,
'Twere idle if we sought,
Or whence her marble vase, by such
Exquisite labor wrought.

Some think it is no earthly thing,
For never yet, they say,
Of earthly birth was seen a flower
With leaves so fair and gay;

And never flower was known to grow
By natural agencies,
Within whose heart 'twere possible
Such wondrous odor lies.

And those who've seen, by rarest chance,
The vase upon the floor,
When warm and bright the sun, at noon,
Streamed through the open door,

Declare the slender fingers clasp
The white and graven heart
So human-like, they cannot be
The work of mortal art.

But whence the flower, or what its name,
    The foolish ones who seek,
For answer have the angry flush
    Upon old Margaret's cheek.

'Tis certain that the plant must link
    Her warped and wandering brain,
To something that is past and gone,
    By a mysterious chain:

And it is well, if e'en in that
    She find a fancied bliss;
For little of the world there seems
    To her, poor soul! but this.

She gathers, through the winter months,
    The snow-flakes as they fall.
And melts them with her breath, to cheer
    Her plant against the wall;

And, in the summer, robs the grass
    Before the sun is hot,
Of sweet and coolest drops of dew
    To feed her marble pot.

While every month, nursed by her care,
    The snow-flakes and the dews,
Her plant, within the broken heart,
    A single flower renews.

And when her flower appears, a change
    Comes over her: she seems
Like one who suddenly awakes
    From wild and troubled dreams.

The lines about her mouth are gone,
    And on her pallid face,
All hushed and calm, you something of
    Its former beauty trace.

The fierceness leaves her eye; her brain
    Grows clearer, and a smile,
That brightens all her haggard face,
    Her shrunken cheeks beguile.

She wraps about her slender form
    A robe of snowy white,
And decks herself with ornaments,
    And colors pure and bright.

She binds a wreath about her brow,
    Her gray and straggling hair
Is neatly braided, and her dress
    Arranged with bridal care.

As by her marble vase she sits,
    Her heart subdued and mild,
She smiles and hums old, simple tunes,
    And calls the flower her child.

And while its fragrance feeds her hear,
    She never leaves her hut,
Her brook creeps on its way alone,
    Her door is always shut.

And nothing then is seen from which
    A passer-by would know
That human soul lived there, except
    Her pathway through the snow,

In winter, to her little brook;
    And, in the summer day,
That to her door a restless foot
    Had worn the grass away.

So still that you can almost hear
    The Snow-flake's fluttering wing,
Or, in her cell, the yellow wasp
    Upon the rafter sing.

One day her flower lives; and when
    Its life, at night, is done,
She sobs and weeps; and as the leaves
    Fall slowly one by one.

She buries them beside the root,
    Last leaf with the last tear!
And waits with patience till again
    Her lost child reappear.

And so her wondrous plant lives on,
  And fades, and blooms again, —
The only thing that can control
  Her dark and wandering brain.

Alas! it is a mournful thing
  A darkened intellect!
A brain so warped and shattered that
  It only can reflect

Disjointed fragments of the light;
  Whose household gods are things
Of fitful fancies, vain designs,
  And false imaginings;

To which, all purpose, object, thought,
  The images it sees,
Are the disordered impulses.
  The forgeries, of Disease.

A fearful thing to see the Mind,
  In its full strength, beset
With swarming shadows, dismal shapes,
  And a base counterfeit

Of Reason all o'ermastering
  Its mighty energies;
While, stricken by its unseen foes,
  The blinded giant lies.

There's no one in the village knows
    Whence the old woman came :
She never told her history,
    Her lineage, or her name.

They called her Margaret ; but why,
    If any knew, they've passed ;
And so, from this, she came to be
    Old Margaret, at last.

Some twenty years, last spring, they say,
    She came into the place,
And through the summer season lived
    By Charity's sweet grace ;

But when the winds grew sharp and chill,
    The elm leaves sere and old,
And Charity's lean hand became
    Few-cented, shy, and cold,

She found the hut below the mill,
    Half fallen from the roof,
Beyond the village and the noise,
    And from the crowd aloof,

And patched it up with moss and slabs,
    To keep the rain away ;

And there, alone, as I have sung,
Has lived unto this day,

This poor and strange old woman,
In the hut below the mill,
Just where the turnpike-road begins
To struggle up the hill.

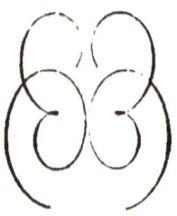

THE FIRST SETTLER.

I.

His hair is white as the winter snow,
His years are many, as you may know,—
    Some eighty-two or three;
Yet a hale old man, still strong and stout,
And able when 'tis fair, to go out
    His friends in the street to see;
And all who see his face still pray
That for many a long and quiet day
    He may live, by the Lord's mercy.

II.

He came to the State when the town was new,
When the lordly pine and the hemlock grew
    In the place where the court-house stands;
When the stunted ash and the alder black,
The slender fir and the tamarack,
    Stood thick on the meadow lands;
And the brook, that now so feebly flows,
Covered the soil where the farmer hoes
    The corn with his hardy hands.

III.

He built in the town the first log hut;
And he is the man, they say, who cut
    The first old forest oak;

His axe was the first, with its echoes rude,
To startle the ear of the solitude,
    With its steady and rapid stroke.
From his high log-heap through the trees arose.
First, on the hills, mid the winter snows.
    The fire and the curling smoke.

IV.

On the land he cleared the first hard year,
When he trapped the beaver and shot the deer,
    Swings the sign of the great hotel ;
By the path where he drove his ox to drink
The mill-dam roars and the hammers clink,
    And the factory rings its bell.
And where the main street comes up from the south,
Was the road he "blazed" from the river's mouth,
    As the books of the town will tell.

V.

In the village, here, where the trees are seen,
Circling round the beautiful Green,
    He planted his hills of corn ;
And there, where you see that long brick row,
Swelling with silk and calico.
    Stood the hut he built one morn :
Old Central Street was his pasture lane.
And down by the church he will put his cane
    On the spot where his boys were born.

VI.

For many an hour I have heard him tell
Of the time, he says, he remembers well,
    When high on the rock he stood,
And nothing met his wandering eye
Above, but the clouds and the broad blue sky,
    And below, the waving wood;
And how, at night, the wolf would howl
Round his huge log-fire, and the panther growl,
    And the black fox bark by the road.

VII.

He looks with pride on the village grown
So large on the land that he used to own;
    And still as he sees the wall
Of huge blocks built, in less than the time
It took, when he was fresh in his prime,
    To gather his crops in the fall;
He thinks, with the work that, somehow, he
Is identified, and must oversee
    And superintend it all.

VIII.

His hair is white as the winter snow,
And his years are many as you may know,—
    Some eighty-two or three;
Yet all who see his face will pray,
For many a long and quiet day
    By the Lord's good grace, that he
May be left in the land, still hale and stout,
And able still when 'tis fair, to go out
    His friends in the street to see.

SCENE IN A VERMONT WINTER.

I.

'Tis a fearful night in the winter-time,
　As cold as it ever can be!
The roar of the wind is heard like the chime
　Of the waves of an angry sea.
The moon is full but the wings, to-night,
Of the furious Blast dash out her light;
And over the sky from south to north,
Not a star is seen, as the storm comes forth
　In the strength of a mighty glee.

II.

All day had the snow come down,—all day,
　As it never came down before,
'Till over the ground, at sunset, lay
　Some two or three feet or more;
The fence was lost, and the wall of stone,
The windows blocked, and the well-curb gone,
The haystack rose to a mountain-lift,
And the woodpile looked like a monster drift
　As it lay by the farmer's door.

As the night set in, came wind and hail,
　While the air grew sharp and chill,
And the warning roar of a fearful gale
　Was heard on the distant hill;
And the Norther! see! on the mountain peak,

In his breath, how the old trees writhe and
    shriek!
He shouts on the plain, "Ho, ho!"
He drives from his nostrils the blinding snow,
    And growls with a savage will.

III.

Such a night as this to be found abroad
    In the hail and the freezing air,
Lies a shivering dog, in the field, by the road,
    With the snow on his shaggy hair:
As the wind drives see him crouch and growl,
And shut his eyes with a dismal howl;
Then, to shield himself from the cutting sleet,
His nose is pressed on his quivering feet:—
    Pray what does the dog do there?

An old man came from the town to-night:
    But he lost the travelled way,
And for hours he trod with main and might
    A path for his horse and sleigh;
But deeper still the snow-drifts grew,
And colder still the fierce wind blew,
And his mare, a beautiful Morgan, brown,
At last o'er a log had floundered down,
    That deep in a hollow lay.

Many a plunge, with a frenzied snort,
    She made in the heavy snow,
And her master urged, till his breath grew short,
    With a word and a gentle blow;

But the snow was deep and the tugs were tight.
His hands were numb and had lost their might;
So he struggled back again to his sleigh,
And strove to shelter himself, till day,
    With his coat and the buffalo.

IV.

He has given the last faint jerk of the rein
    To rouse his dying steed;
And the poor dog howls to the blast in vain,
    For help in his master's need.
For awhile he strives with a wistful cry
To catch the glance of his drowsy eye;
And wags his tail when the rude winds flap
The skirt of his coat across his lap,
    And whines that he takes no heed.

V.

The wind goes down; the storm is o'er;
    'Tis the hour of midnight past;
The forest writhes and bends no more
    In the rush of the sweeping blast.
The moon looks out with a silver light
On the high old hills, with the snow all white;
And the giant shadow of Camel's Hump,
Of the ledge and tree and the ghostly stump,
    On the silent plain are cast.

But cold and dead, by the hidden log,
    Are they who came from the town;
The man in his sleigh, the faithful dog,
    And the beautiful Morgan, brown!

He sits in his sleigh ; with steady grasp
He holds the reins in his icy clasp ;
The dog with his nose on his master's feet,
And the mare half seen through the crusted
  sleet,
Where she lay when she floundered down.

SAN JACINTO.

Vengeance calls you. — quick ! be ready !
    Blood and fortune for the strife !
Gather fast ! be firm and steady !
    Up for freedom ! up for life !
Ho ! be quick ! with bayonet gleaming
    Cover every hill and field ;
See, the tyrant's banner streaming !
    Are ye cowards ? Will ye yield ?

Will ye ? with your brethren gasping
    In the despot's tightening clutch ?
Will ye ? with your old men grasping
    Broken staff and harmless crutch ?
Will ye ? stop a moment ! number
    Those who died where Fanning stood !
The heroes that by Goliad slumber,
    Murdered, weltering in their blood !

Will ye ? hark ! the widow dashes
    From her eye the blinding tear,
And wildly by her children's ashes
    Shrieks for vengeance ; do ye hear ?
Will ye do it ? will ye falter,
    With the struggle so begun ?
Do it, then, and there's the halter !
    Do it ! and your chains are on.

Who will let a tyrant juggle
    Freemen of their birthright? who?
Who wears chains without a struggle?
    Is it you? or you? or you?
Who forgets the men who perish
    In the dungeons of the foe?
By all the hopes that patriots cherish,
    Up! revenge them! rally! ho!

Rouse! hurrah! be quick! be ready!
    Every patriot in his place.
Grasp your chains! be firm! be steady!
    Dash them in the tyrant's face!
Onward! charge from hill and valley;
    On with musket, sword, and pike!
Be your watchward as you rally,
    "Alamo for vengeance! strike!"

PULASKI.

[Count Pulaski fell at the siege of Savannah, in the war of the Revolution. The attack was made on the city, occupied by the English, by the combined forces of the French and Americans, just before daybreak, on the morning of the ninth of October, 1779. Proving unsuccessful, Pulaski, at the head of a company of light horse, attempted to retrieve the fortunes of the day by penetrating a breach into the town. He fell, mortally wounded. His troops, after rescuing his body, retreated, and the siege was abandoned.]

I.

The battle raged ; but they who strove
With tyranny and wrong,
Were struggling vainly in the fight,
A sad and broken throng.

II.

They battled still, though fainter grew
The fierce and desperate charge they made ;
They battled, though the strongest fought
With wearied arm and broken blade.
And weltering on the field in heaps,
Beside their weapons, lay
The lion-hearted troops that led
The fierce and bloody fray ;
Yet still they fought, though vainly still,
Before the leaguered town,
And with the first faint light of morn
The starry flag went down.

III.

"Be ready, now!" cried the gallant Pole,
   As he sprang to his eager steed;
"Be ready, now, in the tyrant's teeth
   One blow for your country's need!"

There's a rush like the wind, and a crash of steel,
As Pulaski's fiery squadrons wheel, —
" Ho for the breach!"
                And on they sweep!
With the flashing shot and the rushing leap;
And everywhere in the thickest storm,
Towers aloft their leader's form;
   And his breast, like a living targe,
Seems to ward the stroke from his struggling band,
As, waving aloft his gleaming brand,
He dashes onward, — loud and clear
O'er the rallying shout, and the leaguers' cheer,
Like a thunder-peal in a summer sky,
Rings his terrible battle-cry, —
   "Pulaski! onward! charge!"

IV.

Hurrah! the flag of the free once more
   Its place in the red van holds!
With the print of the charger's steel-shod hoof,
   And the blood of the foe on its folds.
"Pulaski! on!"

    That cry is heard
Wherever a shout or a fiery word
  Can steady the heart, or nerve the blow :—
"Pulaski! on!"

    And on they go!
Thundering down in their leader's track,
Hurling the ranks of the British back;
And their snorting chargers, dashing through
The broken ranks, as though they knew
That the crushing blow of the riders' might
Was nerved for its deadliest work in the fight,
  With their proud necks arched to the rein,
Rear and plunge with the deadly aim,
As they leap to the breach through the smoke and
  flame,
  And dash o'er the heaps of the slain.

V.

The foe go down by the broadsword's reach,
By the whizzing ball and the pistol's breech;
One sweep, and the blade in the brain is crashed;
One blow, and the corpse in the ditch is dashed;
One thrust, and the hireling's breast is pinned :—
  "Pulaski!"

    Ho! how they quail!
 And at every shout the ranks are thinned
  Like corn by the summer hail.—
"Down with them!"

Fiercer they mix
The cut and the shivering stroke;
And the falling blade leaves a track behind
Like a line of fire in the smoke;
They crowd to the breach, and hand to hand
They level the deadly thrust,
They cheer, they defy, their faces black
With smoke, and with blood and dust.

"Down with the Rebels! back in their teeth
Like hail let the death-shots go!"
"Charge on the Red-coats! trample them
    down!
Down with them! so! and so!
Pulaski-i-i! on! Pulaski-i-i! on
There, now, at the Briton's breast!
Down with them! down! over them there!
Our chargers' heels do the rest!
Pulas — Pulas" — he is down! he is down!
Down in the midst of the swarming foe;
His dread war-cry half breathed on his lips,
And his arm on high for a fearful blow.

VI.

One charge they make, and bear away
Their fallen leader from the fray.
One charge for him, whose plume was tossed
Above the battle fought and lost.

VII.

The fight is done, and the morning sun,
  As it gleams through the battle-smoke,
Reveals the retreat of Freedom's host.
  With their banners rent and their weapons broke.
Slowly they wheel with weary tread
  From the long and fruitless fray;
In silence gathering their spirits up
  For sterner toil on another day.

VIII.

And he who fell, with his faithful blade
  In the wars of Freedom red;
Whose life in her cause was quenched far away
  From the soil where his fathers bled,--
Now sleeps in the land he died to save,
  In the home of the exiled brave;
Sleeps, with a world to tell his fame,
  With a nation's heart for his grave.

THE OLD PINE-TREE.

By my father's house, this side of the hill.
As you followed the road to the cider-mill,
    Was the " swamp," as we called it then,—
A low, wet spot, where the cat-bird mewed,
The tadpole bred, and the bullfrog *spughed*,
    And the muskrat built his den ;
And stealing out from his hiding hole,
Through the rotten grass, came the meadow-mole
    To peep at the works of men.

In the swamp, on a knoll, in the summer dry,
But half-covered up when the springs were high.
    A magnificent Pine had grown :
Last of a race that the State shall see,
Last of his race ! that glorious tree,
    Supreme on his forest throne,
Like a man of strong and wondrous rhyme,
Towering above the rest of his time,
    Stood up in the land alone !

The swamp by the road to the cider-mill,
And the old Pine-Tree, I remember still,
    And well, you will think, I may ;
For there were the boys of the village seen

When the ice was strong, or the leaves were
        green,
    From morn till the night at play,
Skating stones, or rolling the snow
Into cities and forts and castles, you know,
    Or chasing the frogs away.

In winter time, when the snow was deep,
Through the drifts by the old slash-fence they'd
        leap,
    And tumble each other in ;
Then all hands hold, they would " snap the
        snake !" —
How the old " Red Lion" his mane would shake,
    When his prey he chanced to win !
And then, with the old Pine-Tree for a " *gool*,"
They'd play " I-spy " till 'twas time for the school
    In the afternoon to begin.

In the spring when the winter had gone to the
        North,
And the weeds on the knoll came peeping forth,
    And the little wild flowers between,
When the buds swelled out in the April sky,
And the farmer saw that his winter rye
    Came up on the hill-side, green.
From the three-months' school and the ferule free,
With shout and laugh, at the old Pine-Tree
    Again were the boys all seen.

And there on the grass for hours they'd lie,
Making ships and things of clouds in the sky;
    While clear in the fragrant spring,
The bobolink, on the mullein stalk,
Would rattle away like a sweet girl's talk,
    And the gay yellow birds would sing
And chirp to each other with merry call,
As, poised on the top of the milk-weed tall,
    In the wind they reel and swing.

When summer came, and the weeds were thick,
And their blood grew warlike, warm, and quick,
    The train-band company,
With a brake for a plume and a shingle sword,
The gloomy wilds of the swamp explored,
    Their trowsers rolled to the knee;
With broken bricks, and hands full of stones,
At their deadly fire how the cat-tail groans,
    And the hosts of the thistle flee!

'Fore George! what a siege we had one time
With a brave old frog who lived in the slime
    Of a lordly pool at the south!
How he'd dodge out of sight, till our hail had sped,
Then poke up again his great, green head, —
    And wink in the cannon's mouth!
The bricks round his head went thud! thud! thud!
Till the captain lisped, all covered with bl-mud,
    "We can never tear down hith houth."

There many an hour Thanksgiving Day,
When the ice was glare, the girls would stay
    And share in our glorious fun ;
While the shouting boys, with cap in hand,
Would chase them off from the ice to the land,
    Till the Governor's meeting was done ;
Till grace was said, the turkey carved,
The mince-pie cooled and the pudding served,
    And the gravy too cold to run.

They are gone, ah, me! those merry boys,
All gone from the scene of their early joys ;
    Alas, that it should be so!
Some have gone to the West to shake with the
    ague,
And some to the South to die with that plague-
    Y Jack, " Yellow Jack," you know ;
One's made a great spec' in Missouri lead ;
And one, they say, got a broken head
    At the fall of Alamo ;

And one has gone where the soft winds blow
O'er the vine-clad hills of Val d'Arno,
    With his wife, and children two,
And his cheek's regained the glow it lost
In our Northern land of snow and frost ;
    One's in Kalamazoo ;
And one through the drifts of the Northwest snow
Tracks the prairie wolf and the buffalo,
    With a tribe of wild Sioux.

The swamp is ditched: where the leaves used to
    float
A Frenchman has raised some " vary fine oat," —
    The frogs have all hopped off;
And the little green knoll, where the boys used to
    play
Through the spring and the fall and the winter
    day,
    And the cares of manhood scoff,
Is gouged by a premium Berkshire brood,
And the old Pine-Tree by the great high-road
    Is used for a watering trough.

SONG OF THE VERMONTERS BEFORE THE BATTLE OF PLATTSBURGH.

HE who has still left of his two hands but one,
  With that let him grapple a sword;
And he who has two, let him handle a gun;
  And forward, boys! forward! the word.
The murmuring sound of the fierce battle-tide
  Already resounds from afar;
Forward, boys! forward, on every side,
  For Vermont and her glittering star!

Who lingers behind when the word has passed
    down
  That the enemy swarm o'er the line?
When he knows in the heart of a North border-
    town
  Their glittering bayonets shine?
Push on to the North! the fierce battle-tide
  Already resounds from afar;
Push on to the North, from every side,
  For Vermont and her glittering star!

Forward! the State that was first in the fight
  When Allen and Warner were here,
Should not be the last now to strike for the right.
  Should never be found in the rear!

Then, on to the North! the fierce battle-tide
   Already resounds from afar;
Push on to the North, from every side,
   For Vermont and her glittering star!

Hark! booms from the lake, and resounds from
   the land,
The roar of the conflict. Push on!
Push on to the North! on every hand
   Our boys to the rescue have gone;
Forward! the State that was first in the fight
   When Allen and Warner were here,
Should not be the last now to strike for the right,
   Should never be found in the rear.

BARNET.

["So," muttered the dark and musing prince, unconscious of the throng, "so perishes the Race of Iron! Low lies the last baron that could control and command the people. The Age of Force expires with Knighthood and deeds of arms. And over this dead great man I see the New Cycle dawn. Happy, henceforth, he who can plot and scheme, and fawn and smile!" — *Last of the Barons.*]

AND so the Race of Iron passed! —
 So Barnet's bloody field
Saw, cold and still, its lion-heart
 Lie crushed with Warwick's shield.
And when the victor's trumpet rang
 Above his fallen head,
The Age of Knightly Deeds had passed, —
 And Baron-power was dead!

Lord of a hundred baronies!
 Chief of a mighty race!
His lightest word the people's law,
 The throne his knotted mace;
Girt by his more than royal host,
 He heard his war-trump ring,
And towered among his barons bold,
 Too proud to be a king!

But time was working wond'rous change,
 And, from his native realm

Were passing fast the baron's rule,
    The hauberk and the helm.
The land was dealt to nobles new;
    And men of foreign birth
And London loons were swarming round
    The broad old Norman hearth.

His age had perished; and the race
    That gave the age renown
Fell with it, and the Castle bowed
    In silence to the Town:
Low lay its great and mighty chief,
    Its last and noblest man;
And, dawning o'er his broken brand,
    The Age of Trade began.

The age when Barter sneered at Birth,
    And parchment pedigrees
Outweighed the names the Normans bore
    Across the stormy seas;
When shone no more the honest brow
    Beneath the burgonot,
And men began to fawn and smile,
    And cheat, and lie, and plot;

When knaves trod on the knightly heel,
    And avarice, like a rust,
Eat out the brave old chivalry,
    And swords grew thick with dust;
When churls and serfs grew fat with gain,
    And villains bought the land,

And scorned the iron men of yore,
  The battle-axe and brand.

The pen usurped the sword; the loom,
  The mace; the plough, the spear;
And Agriculture cut the grain
  Where rang the battle cheer;
And men began to feel the rule
  Of Trade, more potent grown
Than baron grim, or iron earl,
  Or monarch on his throne.

'Twas best, perhaps: yet from the age
  When trick and traffic came,
When knights turned knaves, and ladies fair
  Grew false to woman's fame;
The age in mincing merchant kings,
  And London Tailors, great —
When craft and cunning, fawn and fraud,
  Began to rule the State, —

We turn, great Baron! to the men
  Who crowned thy regal times!
Admire their rude, gigantic strength,
  And half forget their crimes!
The Castle nursed a mighty race, —
  A race of nature's mould —
And Worth meant something more than Wealth,
  And Grandeur more than Gold.

Those monarch earls and lion lords,
    And barons stout and brave,
Despised the crawling sycophant,
    The sleek and cringing knave!
Their grim, baronial banners told
    Of battles *they* had fought,
Of glory passed from sire to son,
    And not of titles bought!

But trade and traffic, stock and steam,
    The platter and the plough,
The mallet and the milliner,
    Are Lord and Lady now!
The Castle crowns the mousing mart,
    The Palace sails the deep,
Ambition mounts to bantam hens,
    And chivalry to sheep.

The Earl discusses early blues,
    The Baron runs to seed!
And Fame combines a purgative,
    And Skill invents a mead!
Nobility is stock and starch,
    And Greatness fat sirloin,
And Worth and Quality are found
    In calico and coin.

THE OLD AND NEW.

O GENTLE Muse! while still the tale is told
That crowns the dead and glorifies THE OLD,
And books abound in every town and tongue,
Like ancient Herod, death upon the young,
Be ours the song whose sacrilegious rhyme
To newer impulse beats the rapid time:
Let bilious bards, in paralytic verse,
To all the street their dolorous strains rehearse,
Like wandering showmen serve the shivering
    crowds
With nameless mummeries and ghostly shrouds;
We strike the note and sound the bolder lay
That hails THE NEW, and sings the live TO-DAY.

The careful pilot holds with steady force
The bounding vessel to her onward course,
Marks where afar the beacon's warning light
Streams o'er the waters from the distant height,
And learns from maps and ancient charts to
    know
When shoals are near and rocks lie hid below;
But if, when rising storms his skill demand
To sheer the reef and shun the treacherous sand,
The boastful master of his watery realm
Forgets his vessel and neglects his helm,

And gazing backward from his reeling deck
In stupid reverence on the burning speck,
And half-bewildered with his musty chart,
Hears not the storm, nor sees the lightning dart,—
His drifting prow obeys the billow's force,
And howling tempests shape his aimless course.
'Tis well at times, perhaps, to pause and turn
To mark the lights that down the distance burn;
To note what impulse or what hope deceived,
Where error failed and where the truth achieved;
For olden days to ring the sounding chimes,
And bow in homage for the ancient times;
To praise the deeds and glorify the names
That history gathers and tradition claims:
But when 'tis claimed that everything is wrong
Since Hector fought and Homer tuned his song;
That honor, glory, virtue, manhood, pride,
With Pompey perished, with the Cæsar died;
That useless struggles in these modern days
Seek greener laurels, yearn for brighter bays;
That fair is fair because 'tis thick with mould;
That good is only good because 'tis old,—
The Muse shall lift the showy mantle, cast
In reverent folds above the boastful Past;
Reveal the sorrow, bigotry, and wrong
That blot the record and disgrace the song;
Point where, at last, in some poor corner hide
The hero's glory and the conqueror's pride;
And show the gods which modern worship owns,
The pride of Sambo,—half-a-dozen bones.

THE OLD you worship, round whose broken shrine
Your homage trembles and your offerings shine,
How scarred his heart by every sin and shame
By human language honored with a name!
How thick his path with bleaching bones are piled,
With skulls his steps, with blood his hands, defiled!
Round every ruin where the lizard glides,
Through every cavern where the darkness hides,
The halter whitens and the gallows stands,
The torture howls, and gleam the smouldering brands!
There lie the ashes, heaped above the sod,
Where murdered martyrs passed through fire to God;
In vain the bones, still crumbling, seek to hide
The block where saint and brave apostle died;
The cruel cross, the shameful gibbet, tell
Where bled the Christs, and where the prophets fell;
And bones of Genius, which no power could kill,
Rust in their fetters in his dungeons still.
There lies the Worshipped!—robbery and lust,
And blood by ages hardened into crust!
There lies the Reverend!—every daring crime
That blots and blurs the history of time!
This is the god to which you humbly bow,
And these the bays that deck your idol's brow.

Hail to THE NEW! behold her as she stands
Where breaks the morn along the silent sands!
The star that through the night the dawning led,
In radiant glory glitters o'er her head;
She lifts her brow, and, lo! the mists of night
Creep through the valleys from its wondrous
    light;
She waves her hand, the ghosts of many a year
That haunt the present fade and disappear;
And Wrong and Error, long by men misnamed,
Shrink from her presence, naked and ashamed;
While all the life her living breath renews,
From blushing day to evening's glittering dews,—
The falling leaf, the flower that hails the morn,
The winds that wave the tassels of the corn,
The song of birds, the shoot of waterfalls,
The thousand wings that glance along the walls;
And spring and hope, and all things rich and
    rare
That love the earth or sweep the liquid air,—
Like troops of children on the lawn at play,
Cling to her robe, and dance along the way.
THE OLD, exhausted, weak and worn at last,
No future hoping, living in the past,
Turns sadly back his dim and weary eye
Where love and hope in mournful records lie;
By foiled endeavor, broken strength, oppressed,
For quiet yearns, and sighs to be at rest:
Or, idly musing over broken schemes,
Like one remembering half-forgotten dreams,
Worn with his grief, and trembling with his fears,

Weeps o'er the graves of all his fallen years :
So the pale mourner, lingering by the tombs
Till ghostly midnight o'er the landscape glooms,
While through the clouds the moon's uncertain
    light
Shows now the darkness, now the headstone
    white,
Stands trembling as the mournful winds that pass
Lift the light leaf and stir the murm'ring grass,
And, shuddering at the shapes his fancy weaves,
Shrinks from the shadows and the rustling leaves.
THE NEW, all life and vigor, laughs to scorn
The chattering ghosts of age and darkness born,
Her healthy nerves disdain the idle fears,
The wandering shapes a sickly fancy rears ;
No ghostly stone, no pale sepulchral light,
Deludes her sense, or scares her fearless sight.
Far to the future, lo ! her daring eye
Sweeps the horizon, pierces to the sky ;
Her restless energy all this essays,
No struggle hinders and no force delays ;
Bold, confident, and daring, to her track,
Where Faith grows dizzy and where Hope looks
    back !
She robs the earth of treasures hid below,
In cunning coffers, centuries ago ;
Dares her bold course where fabled rivers roll,
And seas lie frozen round the Northern pole ;
Wrings from the sea the wrecks by tempests
    strown ;
Invades the sun upon his regal throne ;

Hails to the coming years that, dark and dim,
Lie far and pale on the horizon's rim ;
And, sweeping on through realms of brooding
    Night,
Drags hidden worlds and trembling stars to light.
THE OLD, in mind, religion, science, law,
Sees only what the reverend fathers saw ;
Still loves the forms, and still adores the pride,
By custom sanctioned and by usage tried ;
Still fearing only restless change to see,
Content if only what has been may be :
THE NEW denies the laws and forms that bind
To things that were, the muscle or the mind ;
Scorns mouldy compacts, sneers at musty rules,
Laughs at your edicts, and defies the schools ;
And bravely battling with all sodden creeds,
Your worshipped idols and your gilded deeds,
Against the bulwarks of established things
Her cannon thunders and her falchion rings ;
And, where the world in bigotry has nursed
A bloated custom or a law accursed,
Hurls her wild strength, and swings her fearful
    might,
To crush the Wrong and vindicate the Right.
She builds your monuments, she carves your
    stones,
She rears the marble o'er the martyr's bones ;
She piles the granite where the hero lies,
She lifts the column where the patriot dies,
She weaves the halo round the prophet's head,
She bids us weep where all the good have bled ;

She keeps the ashes, garners all the tears,
Where Genius perished, and where wept the seers;
She lights the dungeon grim with hoary moss,
She gilds the block and consecrates the cross.
THE NEW redeems and purifies THE OLD!
Observe the oak in autumn, and, behold!
When frosts appear and through the withered leaves
The long night darkens and November grieves,
The sap will leave its chilled and naked form
To all the scourges of the wintry storm,
The bitter tempest and the howling blast
Pluck from its frozen hands the ripened mast;
Through mournful months they lie beneath the snow,
While rains descend and freezing winters blow.
But Spring revives the cold and sluggish blood,
Redeems the leaf, and swells the shrunken bud:
And life, from sullen death renewing still,
Crowns with new oaks the valley and the hill.
From all the death that wastes the buried heart,
New flowers appear and fresher leaves will start;
The fallen beauty and the dark decay,
O'er which December mourns, the smile of May
Renews again, and, bursting from the tomb,
See fairer forms and brighter glories bloom.
Lo! when the scourge on all the city falls,
And ghostly shadows throng deserted walls,
When all our skill the pestilence defies,
Dries up the blood and wastes the glazing eyes,

Far from the forest where the healthful breeze,
In playful circles stirs the Northern seas.
THE NEW, rejoicing, speeds her hopeful way,
With cooler nights and fresher, purer day.
When all the summer months grow hot and dry,
And burning suns flame down a brazen sky;
When lakes lie shrunken in their narrow shores,
And brooks no longer murmur by the doors ;
When faints the river, and its sickly strength
Scarce round the pebble drags its shallow length ;
When noons are burning, and the nights refuse
The cooling zephyr and the balmy dews ;
When pools grow noisome, stagnant waters breed
The wasting scourge, and deadly fevers feed, —
At midnight, lo! the dark and troubled West
Glooms with the storm that rears its billowy crest,
And far along, the wide old forest through,
The morning hails the purifying NEW.
The gathered blasts she pours along the seas,
And hurls the winds against the groaning trees,
Cleaves through the land, and on the grateful
 plain
Descends in floods of cool and healthful rain.
THE OLD, at times, grows insolent and strong,
Defies the world with every hated wrong !
His hissing rods, with fierce and grim delight,
The naked necks of cowering nations smite ;
While loud and sad, the pale and weeping land
Groans with the scourge that smites her lifted
 hand.
Hark to the shout that rings along the plains !

Aroused at last, THE NEW has crushed her chains,
And, sweeping onward like the fearful roar
When summer whirlwinds up the valley pour,
Her knotted fists, her howling millions shake,
And fearful vengeance on oppression take.
In righteous judgment on the bloated Wrong,
With power grown insolent, with murder strong,
Stripped to the retribution as she bends,
The torture hisses and the scourge descends.
The fest'ring ulcers, that had grown, at length.
A wasting drainage of the nation's strength,
Gangrened, offensive, that for years had passed
All peaceful remedy, her sword, at last,
Leaps to its poise, — like light descends, and, lo!
Cuts from the morbid system at a blow.

'Tis passing strange, the Muse reluctant sings,
The love of some for old and rotten things.
Before his flock the reverend pastor stands,
The quiet sheep are feeding from his hands,
Dried herbs! from which a thousand years of rust
Have cut the life, and left them crumbling dust;
No living leaf, no spear of grass is seen,
'Twould hardly seem could ever have been green.
His audience sit in dull respectful seats,
While musty saws the orator repeats,
And closing off with golden glories fled,
With cycles finished and with systems dead,
Bids all the world, in vapid strains, behold
How great the Past, how very wise THE OLD.

Grim War once more has dashed his iron heel
Upon the nations ; thrones and kingdoms reel ;
From out the record with a lawless hand
He tears the names of empires, in the sand
Stamps out the lines of old dominions ; pours
His swart and howling legions like the roar
Of whirlwinds in the valley ; from the hill
Boom the loud thunders of his savage will ;
Forward ! and in the name of truth and God
He grapples with the old and blood-stained rod.
How firm his red hand grasps the glittering sword !
How fiercely on he cheers his savage horde !
How follow on his carnage mute Despair !
How loathsome Death, and Fire with streaming hair !

. . . . . .

THE OLD has fallen ! and THE NEW, its law
Fulfilled ; and those who understood it saw
The millions, in their fearful anger, rise,
With huge bare arms, knit brows, and glaring eyes,
Against oppression's rusted bars, and dash
Them down forever ; — saw in the days that splash
The heaven with blood a whole accursed race
Of tyrants strangled at a grasp ; the embrace
Of Force and Ignorance torn apart, and blows
Dealt justly out against unrighteous foes. '
THE NEW has passed a fierce and bloody day ;
And yet the fire, though scathing, cleared away
The mouldering old opinions, wrongs that lay

Like millstones on the people's palsied strength.
The festering ulcer, that had grown at length
So gangrened and offensive, and had passed
All peaceful remedy, the sword at last
Has scalpelled from the system; and the men
Beneath whose frown the world shook as the glen
Cowers in the shadow of the hills; whose lives
For centuries had been sapless, and whose gyves
And fetters had been worn, because the slaves
Who wore them deemed that they to lords and knaves
Were born to pander, nor had dreamed the power
That slumbered in their sinews, till the hour
When, mighty as the fabled voice of Thor,
Clanged in their ears the brazen peal of War, —
Bed-ridden, palsied men, worm-eaten, dead,
Cumb'ring God's heritage; the bolt that sped
Dashed them to earth: as in the forest, see!
Towering aloft, some huge o'ershadowing tree,
Whose rotten heart no sap for years has nursed,
The storms that darkly from the heavens burst
Whirl to the ground its useless bulk; the blast,
With its war strength, accomplishes at last
What years of peaceful sunshine, quiet rain,
And slow decay, had striven to do in vain.
The learned doctor cures our mortal ills
With father's plasters and with gran'ther's pills.
"We're all," he says, "so very near the same,
There's need to change the physic but in name;"
And gravely dosing as the books declare,
A blister here, a pill or powder there,

Relieves the liver, lets the lazy vein,
Just as they did in Doctor Galen's reign.
And where in law our modern practice storms
The stilted customs or established forms,
The staid old lawyer, stiff with starch and time,
Shows his contempt ineffably sublime,
Abates your writ, declares your pleading dead,
If, in the whole, you've missed a single *said*.
The poet tunes his harp, and ancient times,
Like moss and weeds, lie tangled in his rhymes;
And soft his simple sonnet sighing swells
Of nameless nymphs and dear delightful dells,
Exciting maids with heat from wasted flames,
And ancient men with ghosts of ancient dames.
He mourns the times, now lost in endless night,
When god and goddess blest our mortal sight;
And dreaming still of soft Elysian days,
To whittling Yankees tunes Arcadian lays.
The mighty member from his native town,
Wrapped in his linen and his suit of brown,
Mourns for the seat where, forty years before,
The people sent his ancestors to snore;
Tells how his gran'ther, in his homespun drabs,
Sat out the session on a seat of slabs; —
Scowls at the varnish and the pictured wall,
The sure forerunner of the nation's fall;
Shakes his bald head, and flaps his lengthened ear,
Where modern fops the granite columns rear,
And, firm against such wastefulness and show,
Hurls his bad English and his thundering No!

E'en Fashion stoops to train her flowers and
    fold,
In humble reverence for the sainted OLD ;
And we who once could dare to risk a guess
What motive-power controlled the moving dress,
Behold it now, with trailing length of skirt,
Dragged like great Hector in ignoble dirt,
And find our streets, in sunny afternoons,
A waving mass of family balloons ;
The snowy robe, that round her bosom steals,
Heaves with the Beauty whom it half conceals,
Who, strangely modest, when she stems the street
Strips half her person to conceal her feet ;
Bare in the sun, to all the gaping town
She hides the bonnet and displays the crown ;
And sweetly deigns, in all her pride to stoop,
Like Sioux chiefs, to glory in a (w)hoop.

There's worth to some — so far their reverence
    goes —
In napless beavers and in seedy clothes ;
No name a thought, no history a word,
By palsy threatened nor by wrinkle blurred ;
Of war afraid, they start and shrink with pain
Where searching lancets find an oozing vein ;
No hope, alas! from anything derive
By age left breathing, or by time alive ;
For modern days, so great their nervous fears,
So deep their reverence for THE OLD appears,
Like frightened children, lost among the firs,
They shudder if they touch a thing that stirs.

New men, new things, new movements, they
    abjure,
These from the past the fickle crowd may lure;
Abhorring notions, manners, customs, all
Whose date they trace this side of Adam's fall,
They curse the law, refuse to hear the creed
Not having run a century to seed,
And, looking wise, pronounce your genius base
If royal George disdain a dirty face.
So full of reverence for THE OLD, they trace
A mould or wrinkle as a special grace;
Regretting when they see the look of new,
From Cheshire cheese to some religious view;
They choose alike their sirloin and their saint
Less for their virtue than their ancient taint;
Preferring, when their gastric juice they suit,
A speck of rotten in their autumn fruit.
You broach a subject, you suggest a view, —
The answer's ready, — " Bah! the thing is new!"
You write a song, you make a plough or book, —
Be careful, friend, it has a newish look!
A grand discovery the Nation hails!
The noisy shout all fogydom assails!
And gathering round, in shy and nervous bands,
All half-distracted, peer through trembling hands:
" All folly! folly! worse than folly, — dross!
I see no rust about it, there's no moss!"
Advance your proposition. — " Sir, I say,
I know how 'tis: I'm wise, of course; I'm gray!"
Produce your reasons, and at once you're told,
If they're a little knotty. " Sir, I'm old!"

And, if a moment standing to your pride,
You dare defend, and, worse, dispute beside,
To end the strife, the last grand stroke employ,
They shake their hoary locks, and call you *Boy!*
Advance is sinful, and all progress wrong,
All new discoveries but an evil throng :
The scholar, searching through the mazy creeds
To glean the wheat among the lusty weeds ;
The genius, watching through the starry night
For newer glories and more radiant light,
In jumbling books by hoary ages sealed,
And seeking what is not to be revealed ;
The sager science that inspires the age
Blasts all the land with infidelic rage ;
Grim Mathematics, crazy with her signs,
Through Pluto's regions runs her impious lines ;
While bold Astronomy, with curves and cubes,
Glares into heaven through her brazen tubes ;
The rumbling engine and the rushing car
Wage on the Past a sort of impious war ;
And, lo! in Fulton's glory, hissing steam,
A fettered devil shouting in his dream ;
To sail through space without a wing, alas!
When understood, is scaling heaven with glass ;
And strangely daring the electric fire,
To write by lightning with a common wire.
Not to be old and half-obscured by time,
Is always folly, frequently a crime ;
Nothing that's old can ever need defence,
And want of age is always want of sense ;

Their squinting vision, blurred and flat with
    years,
Discerns the best what farthest off appears:
'Tis always something safely kept in dust;
'Tis always something sacred in its rust;
Some ancient name, whose phosphorescent light,
Like rotten wood, shines only in the night;
Some mighty deed, that held to modern view,
Grins grim defiance to the groping NEW.
And so 'tis always, when THE NEW appears,
The bigot OLD receives the child with sneers;
Who can be great that every day we meet?
How prophet he who lives across the street?
" That drivelling idiot! — let the fool be bound!
The noisy babbler says the world is round!"
" That imp of Satan! seize, or we are lost!
And all the gods protect us from this Faust!"
" Columbus! hear him, mighty dons of Spain!
New worlds, he says, lie hid across the main!"
" Ye learned doctors! reverèd since the Flood!
Hear crazy Harvey preach about the blood?
What strange delusions! what an idle dream!
Propelling boats and factories by steam!
And here's a man — to what strange things we
    come! —
Corks lightning as a grocer corks his rum!"
And so 'tis always, priest or prophet sent
To heal the land, and bid the world repent,
THE OLD, indignant when a newer light
Dawns on the world, and pains his shrivelled
    sight.

Besotted, ignorant, self-sufficient, vain,
Fights everything that cuts his bloated reign,
And praising still, with paralytic awe
Some dotard hero or some rotten law,
Bends meekly down to kiss the graven stone,
And rises up to crucify his own.

'Tis well, indeed, 'tis well to reverence age,
To crown the locks that grace the tottering sage;
But vain the task, with leaves however green,
To hide the snows that time reveals between.
With the dark locks that graced her waiting-maid,
Her faded brow the waning belle may shade,
And, when the lamp deludes the dazzled sight,
May glow with rouge, and gleam with lily white;
The faded fop among the crowd may glide,
His hair be-Bogled, and his whiskers dyed:
But truthful Day disdains the shallow feint,
Reveals the barber, and displays the paint.
It may be well with sober steps to tread
Where mould'ring greatness fills its narrow bed;
Around the idol wrapped in awe to kneel,
The fault to cover and the sin conceal.
But, gild the shrine however much we may,
Howe'er so deep our reverent homage pay,
Time slowly crumbles all the blocks we rear
To mark the tomb and consecrate the bier.
And Truth at last, stern justice on her lips,
Disrobes the idol, and the altar strips.

Still, hail THE NEW when sigh the summer bowers,
The robin warbles, and descend the showers,
Where drifts the bark on far Dakotah's shores,
Or Arabs wander where the Jordan pours,
Where Winter reigns along the Northern seas,
Or glows the orange in the tropic breeze,
Where cities swarm, or burns the barren steep,
Whese deserts lie, or green savannahs sweep,
Wherever life in all its varied forms
Glows in the sun or freezes in the storms.
Her radiant beauty blushes in the buds,
Swells in the breeze, and murmurs in the floods,
And when THE OLD, at last, grows dim and gray,
Shrinks from the sunshine and abhors the day,
His pulse grown feeble, and his glowing eye
Proclaims the edict, It is time to die;—
THE NEW, all radiant with her glorious life,
Wings her soft way to cheer the closing strife;
Sits by his pillow in the mournful hours,
With fragrant presence, and with bursting flowers;
Wipes from his brow the clammy dews of death;
Steals with soft lips his last expiring breath;
Lays the green sod upon his silent heart;
Rears o'er his sleep the sculptured tears of art;
And on his grave, where loving memories cling,
Renews the blossoms of eternal Spring.

LIFE'S MISSION.

Behind the hills, his daily journey done,
Descends again the slowly setting Sun.
The clouds, at dawn that met his earliest smile,
Ere flamed his glance along the distant isle,
Flung their white banners round his burning way
When glowed the heavens with his meridian ray,
Stirred by the Winds, whose wings their slumbers
    fret,
Unveil their idol ere his glory set:
His flaming circle sinks beyond the eye,
Though still his radiance lingers in the sky;
As when at last creation's work was done,
And he along the glowing heavens had won
His first full journey, and the starry Night
Stole up the East to watch his parting light.
Note we, in this departure of the Sun,
No meaning save that he again has run
His daily passage? Is there nothing more
Than that his smile is gone, and day is o'er?
He left the hills upon his destined way,
As you may mark he leaves them every day,
And nothing new or strange to-night appears;
The same his course as for six thousand years:
Along the valley and the distant shore
The shadows thicken, and the day is o'er;
The hills against the sky stand like a wall.

The stars again appear; and is this all?
Ah, no! beyond his setting in the skies
A deep significance, though silent, lies;
He has fulfilled his mission, — clear and bright
The clouds you saw retain his glowing light
With half of noon's magnificence, and throw
Their softened influence on the plain below,
Wreathed round his setting while the heavens
　　were stilled,
To crown that mission faithfully fulfilled.

There are, if we will notice, men who dream
That what they note is only what they seem;
Who only mark the visible, the form, —
The tree, the bud, the flower, the rain, the
　　storm, —
The tokens merely, of the indwelling Power
That manifests itself in tree and flower;
The mere development, and not the life
With which all these developments are rife.
The heavens above, the teeming earth below,
To these are but a grand and gorgeous show,
A splendid pageant and unmatched display,
Magnificent phenomena, they say.
In all the various forms of life they see
No other end or purpose than to be.
The death that blasts, the war that desolates,
The storm that rends, the strife that shatters
　　states,
Are accidents that mournfully befall, —
Afflictions merely, incident to all.

They are not wise who only this discern,
Who nothing deeper than results can learn.

 The noisome thistle, growing by the road,
Whose drifting seed the wind each year has sowed;
The lordly oak, whose proud and haughty form
Defies at night the fury of the storm;
The breeze, that wakes the robin's sleep at morn,
And plays among the tassels of the corn;
The cruel hail, that cuts the forest leaves,
Destroys the grain, and blasts the gathered sheaves;
The silent rain, that in the midnight hour
Distils its freshness on the meadow flower;
The music of the wild bee's drowsy hum,
When columbines and honeysuckles come;
The bird, that hops and twitters on the snow,
When winds are cold and bitter tempests blow;
The storm, that, rising, darkens all the hills,
And sounding seas with shuddering terror fills;
The swelling waves, that hail and kiss the sky,
Or round the continents in slumber lie;
The worm, along the sand that scarcely crawls,
On whose dull form the careless footstep falls, —
Each has, obeying sweetest order still,
Its own peculiar mission to fulfil.
Through all the wide and far-extending range
Of these developments, however strange,
Are fixed and certain purposes that lie
Below the surface and beyond the eye.
There's not a flower, there's not a slender blade

That lives beneath the locust's quiet shade,
The frailest, most unnoticeable leaf,
With use most doubtful, and with life most brief;
There's not a storm that blasts the summer grain;
There's not a strife that gloats above its slain, —
But has a meaning deeper than appears
Upon the surface of their narrow spheres, —
A meaning deeper than the shocks that jar,
The frosts that blacken, and the deaths that mar.
Beside the road the traveller turns to taste
The bubbling spring that cheers the arid waste;
The silent dews, the gentle summer rains,
Nurse the sweet flowers that bless the barren
    plains;
The Breeze, at noon, from out the slumb'rous
    shade,
Where Labor faints upon the stifled glade,
Fans the scorched meadows with its cooling wings
Dipped in the spray of running brooks and
    springs;
And when the growing shadow of the hills
Spreads o'er the plain and all the valley fills,
The Zephyr wanders from the sea to play
Among the fragrant grass and ripened hay,
Cools the hot cheek with burning fever dried,
Steals through the half-drawn curtain to the side
Of patient Sickness, to the cradle creeps
Where Childhood on its moistened pillow sleeps,
And through the open door-way to his chair,
To gladden Age and stir his frosty hair.
Mark how each season passes on; how true

Each to its mission, — sunshine, cloud, and dew,
Frost, storms, and drifting tempests, in their sphere,
Fulfil their cheerful task from year to year.
Bleak Winter, when the gentle flowers are dead,
Throws his white mantle o'er each fallen head,
Invigorates their strength, till sweeter dew
And kindly winds their fresher life renew :
And Spring, with beaming smile and genial breath,
Dispels the shades and gloomy damps of death ;
In valleys green, beneath the maple shade,
Calls forth the blossom and the shooting blade :
Warm Summer brings the hot and blazing morn,
With blooming clover and with waving corn,
Rears the tall grass along the mowers' glade,
And shields the traveller with the thickened shade ;
And Autumn fills the store with ripened grain.
While sings the reaper on the fruitful plain ;
Heaps the ripe fruit where Labor's basket stands.
And fills with golden corn the husker's hands.

And man, too, has his mission : in the hall
Or hovel, whereso'er his lot may fall,
Despised or courted, glorified or blamed,
With honor loaded or with hatred named,
In rags or linen, sorrow, fear, or joy,
In manual labor or in soft employ, —
Life has a meaning deeper than appears
Upon the record of our threescore years.

Below its surface, which the strong winds curl,
Where rocks divide and angry eddies whirl,
What earthly intellect, what wisdom knows,
The purpose of the mighty stream that flows?
From out the hollow of the Almighty's hand
It issues, and the boundary of its strand,
Sweeping beyond the age of burning spheres,
Fades in the circle of eternal years.
And being here to work, to live, to die,
Doth more than merely being signify;
And man's existence, with its hopes and fears,
From youth's fresh buds to age's hoary years,
Should in itself to him be something more
Than idle pastime on an ocean's shore;
Than blowing bubbles filled alone with air;
Or chasing butterflies with childish care;
Than moulding, throughout all his busy day,
Some image of himself in potter's clay;
Than seeking, even from his mother's breast,
Of lands and halls and dust to be possessed;
Than following the vain and idle shows
That gilded power and worldly honor knows;
Than yearning for the sounding names that grace
" The pomp of circumstance, the pride of place;"
Or seeking from the throngs that crowd the way
The fickle tides and changes of the day,
The short-lived homage and the trustless power
That crown the idol of the passing hour.
These trifles, and the pageantry that decks
The conqueror's bloody triumphs, and the wrecks

On which Ambition builds his haughty throne
With brazen monuments and chiselled stone ;
The gilded trappings, and the power that falls
To wealth and fashion and to marble halls,—
Are but the husks that rattle round the ear
When harvest-time has crowned the ripened year.
Yes! man for nobler things than these was lent ;
Of life the most complete development,
His being has a mission further still
Than the mere record of life's good or ill.
And he may learn from merely outward forms,
From faithful seasons and from fruitful storms,
From glowing sunsets and from changing year,
His duty to his mission in his sphere.
The storms, the rain, the floating clouds that bar
The heavens from his vision, every star,
The spring-time with its promise, and the fall
With its fulfilment,—these will each and all
Be teachers to him, and the earth and sky
Perpetual lessons to his inner eye.
Each has his mission, and no one can shirk
The duties of his own appropriate work.
In this, there falls to man nor golden mean,
Division neither, neither hope to lean
Upon his erring brother ;—but each has his own
Peculiar sphere, in hovel or on throne ;—
A work to do, a labor to fulfil ;
In its fulfilment lies his good or ill !
And he who paves with stones the streets we
    tread ;
Who frames the roof for shelter o'er the head ;

Who digs the earth, or earns from day to day
His coarse and scanty food, as best he may,—
If faithful to his place, in all his ways,
To him, as much, in his own sphere, be praise
As to his brother who a world commands,
Or in the forum or the senate stands.
Yes! he who nobly fills his destined place,
With patient labor and with quiet grace,
Who in his sphere works out his destined part
With genuine purpose and with loyal heart,
To him, and not to ribbons, white or blue,
The honor of a faithful man is due.

In all our life-work it were well to pause
And note how to the universal laws
By which all things are governed, in the round
Of never-ending struggle, each is found
Harmonious, submissive, laboring still
Its own peculiar duty to fulfil.
How faithful Summer in the quiet glade
Waits for the clover and the growing blade!
And how to crown the fully-ripened year,
Doth Autumn tarry for the yellow ear!
And how his freezing breath doth Winter seem
To hold, till on the hillside by the stream
The little autumn flower has had its day,
Fulfilled its silent work and passed away!
Each has its own appropriate duty! Dwells
The Summer in the coolness of the dells
To judge the Autumn? Doth the Autumn wail
To chide the Winter with a lagging gale?

And doth the Winter, with his hoary head.
Condemn the Spring because she doth not shed
Her flowers upon his snow-drifts? And doth she
Upbraid his stormy brow and boisterous glee,
Because, forsooth, he doth not choose to bear
Her buds and blossoms in his frosty hair?
Flaunts the red Sun his fierce and haughty eye
Upon the pale Moon trembling in the sky?
Her glory full, and through the harvest night
Alone, she reigns the peerless queen of light;
Bends she her brow in scorn, because the Star,
When her dim crescent crowned the hills afar,
That on his path the weary traveller cheers,
In her full glory pales and disappears?
In boist'rous anger doth the great Sea rail
Against the Lake that in the narrow vale,
A handful of sweet waters, meekly lies
Among the lilies where the wild bird flies?
The monarch River struggling with the Shore,
That Cataract, with its eternal roar,
The one does not begrudge the Rill that creeps
Among the alder-roots, and softly sleeps
Through all the sultry summer days that pass,
Beneath the yellow weed and waving grass!
Nor doth the other scorn the Brook that falls
From where a child may reach, and shouts and calls
With prattling clamor all the woods to tell
How dizzy was the height it leaped so well!
Who listens when the Night broods on the lake
Hears not the Primrose taunt the ragged Brake;

The Buttercup, the Thistle; Lilies blown,
The dull and senseless Moss upon the stone:
And we who note these, truth from them may
 read,
A lesson it were well for us to heed :—

Judge not thy brother: there may be
More of the man in him than thou canst see.
Pray, is the wretched child at fault because
His birth had not the sanction of the laws?
Is he at fault because he was begot
By satined villain or by ragged sot?
He, if he could have willed his sire or birth,
Had not been beggar-boy upon the earth;
He, if he could have governed this before,
Had not been begging crusts from door to door:
But some proud lord, with sounding name, had
 smiled
Upon his cradle-place, and called him child.
Hast thou discovered all the various laws
Of thy humanity, and is the cause
And purpose of thy being made so plain
To thee, when others seek to know in vain,
That thou canst say to all life's motley throng,
Who worketh not as *I* work worketh wrong?
Who gave to thee the power to comprehend
The mission of thy brother, and the end
For which *he* labors? and how happen you
To have an eye that, penetrating through
The Almighty's secret plans, hath power to tell
Whether thy brother worketh ill or well?

How this thing sounds to him, or that appears,
How canst thou tell without his eyes and ears?
The beggar-boy and fatherless you meet,
Half-starved and naked, wandering through the street,
Whose birth was in a hovel, and who knows
No more of sin than of the wind that blows,
With sunburnt face, and bare and blistered feet,
The jeer of crowds, the laughter of the street,
He gnaws the broken offal,—oh, beware,
How falls thy hand upon his matted hair!
Sick, sad, and weary, how his pleading eye
Asks for the charity your hands deny!
While in the distance which you do not see,
Fame smiles to note your answer to his plea;
Or sits the recording angel, turned to hear
And note thine answer, with a smile or tear.

'Tis hard to tell, of all the throng we meet,
As day by day we pass along the street,
When future generations come to make
The record of the present, who will take
The crown of glory; who, at last, have won
The laurel wreath for works most nobly done.
From out the gloom and night that lies beyond,
What says the Past? we wave the magic wand:
Before the eye, the clouds their darkness lift;
And moving, see, they slowly upward drift!
What shapes are these?—a strange and motley band

Press through the shades that shroud the silent
    land.
Behold, and wondering smile to see who claim
The wreath of fame and boast a living name :
Now, one by one, they're moving by,—alas !
See what strange shadows and what spectres pass !
A sturdy butcher leads the awkward train ;
A ploughman, dripping with the autumn rain ;
A cobbler, bent with toil and worn with years ;
And there ! a tailor passes with his shears ;
A blacksmith there, still grim from forge and shop ;
And that ! a barber with his brush and strop ;
A weaver bears his shuttle through the throng ;
A tinker's son stalks silently along.
The shrinking scholar, whose unnoticed life
Casts not a shadow on the world of strife
While marshalled legions wheel along the morn,
In some cold cell with hope and study worn,
His name unknown, and scarce his home or clime,
May sit *the* foremost man of all his time.
Day after day, with purpose strong and brave,
He casts his thoughts abroad upon the wave ;
No resting-place for them in all the land,
They flutter back to nestle in his hand.
His hero-heart ! complaints nor murmurs rise ;
In patient faith he does his work and dies ;
The overseers lay his bones to rest
In rudest coffin and in coarsest vest,
And, turning on his grave their reverend backs,
Count so much less of annual pauper-tax ;
Yet when the future hastens to decide

On our pretensions, our expectant pride.
Look upward! higher! on the roll of fame
The sun, at morn, strikes first upon his name.
'Tis still remembered how a man was seen
Bending, at midnight, o'er a strange machine,
Begrimed with dirt, oppressed with want and scorn,
Judged by the old a crazy dreamer born ;
The shapeless model which his hands have wrought
To realize a vast and mighty thought,
On which to waste a life of want and care
More useless seems than bubbles of the air ;
And those who watched his patient toil and slow,
And heard at night his ever-restless blow,
Shook their wise heads in pity for his kind
Of feebled intellect and darkened mind.
Yet still he labored, still his trembling hand
Forged clasp and pivot, drew the iron band ;
And still at night, upon his sleepless bed,
Clung his loved idol to his aching head.
This idle dream, of sick delusion born,
By his own generation laughed to scorn,
Now whirls the car along the levelled sands,
Bears the broad commerce of the farthest lands,
And scorning winds, defying storm and breeze,
Breasts the blue billows of a thousand seas.

Time makes sad changes ; and, alas, how few
Their busy lives to after years renew !
The men to whom the world has bent the knee,

Whose flags have waved o'er every land and sea,
With vast report of deeds from year to year
Have filled and stunned their generation's ear.
How smooth the waters o'er their glories close!
How dark the night that shrouds their dull repose!
The lonely dweller in some narrow vale,
Far from the noise, who, fainting, sick, and pale,
Turns from his task his dim and weary eye
To mark the idol of his time go by,
Now raises in the distance, through the storm
And cloud and shadow of the past, his form;
Towers like a mountain on a distant cape
By thunders rent and worn to human shape!
Some who nor form nor power nor honor boast,
By after ages may be honored most;
Some whose ignoble brain seems warped and numb,
Whose tongues are speechless, and whose lips are dumb,
Their form at last, when they their crown have won,
Fills all the heaven with glory like the sun.
Who piled the pyramids with anxious aim
Upon the world to stamp a deathless name?
None answer,—even Rumor has grown dumb;
While restless traveller and scholar come,
And more the glory now to him who reads
The doubtful record of forgotten deeds,
Than to the men whose vain ambition sent
To heaven the gray and towering monument.
Gigantic on the desert seas they stand!

They shade the camel and o'erlook the sand!
The builders from the world the doubt have won,
By whom completed or by whom begun.
The gaping wonder what would men beguile
To vex the future with the useless pile.
When from the North the rude barbarian rushed,
With conquest drunken and with victory flushed;
When to oppose his wild and swarming train
One-half the world seems camped upon the plain,
The mighty Tartar led his furious clan,
Swung his red axe upon the reeling van,
And, overwhelmed, the opposing hosts have fled,
And left behind their pyramids of dead,—
Who dreamed, as then the mighty conqueror
    stood,
His horse's fetlock deep in human blood,
A German boy with printer's block would rear
A prouder glory than the Tartar's spear?
How many who have sat in grand estate,
Bepraised and lauded by their times as great,
Come down to us as living at the time
When some poor witling wrote his idle rhyme?
How many a king immortal fame has gained
From boors and barbers, christened when they
    reigned!
"She hardly thought the man who wrote her
    plays,
From her proud name would steal the future gaze!
That on the page, her fame would be the note,
'She ruled the realm, while Master William
    wrote;'"

'Tis hard to tell where Glory claims her own,—
Whether they grace the hovel, hall, or throne.
But Time decides the right, it will be seen,
With an impartial hand decides between
Galileo's crazy dream and Charlemagne,
The types of Faust. the spear of Tamerlane.

The true man never fails! his life may be
The weariest years of woe and poverty:
Though darkness hover o'er his way, and doubt
And persecution hedge his path about;
Though Bigotry's black anger, and the clogged
And blundering tongue of Ignorance. and dogged
Opinion's sullen eye: the zealot's ire,
Oppression's rack, Fanaticism's fire,—
Cast over him their shadows black and grim.
To paralyze his heart and rack his limb:
Yet, let him labor on with honest zeal,
In poverty or wealth, in woe or weal:
He never fails; for what beneath the sun
Was set for him to do, is truly done.

Man's being hath a mission that the grasp
Of world-wide empires, and the jewelled clasp
Of diadems about his brow, the toil
For far dominion, and the ill-gotten spoil
Of countless kingdoms, and the humbled pride
Of conquered nations bending by his side,
Will not accomplish: 'twill not do to heap
Ambitious thrones together, nor to steep
His spirit in debaucheries, and stain

His heart with evil passions, in the vain
And foolish hope to smother in his soul
Its awful purpose. He cannot control
The subtle influences that everywhere
Remind him of his manhood : shall not dare
To disregard it ; shall not seek to hush
Its stern demands upon him, or to crush
Its solemn dictates. Gather round thy state
The cares and schemes and sorrows of the great ;
Turn to thy slumber on a regal bed,
When one more day of golden pomp has sped.—
It will not answer : it is with thee still,
Thy work to do, thy mission to fulfil.
Forget thy manhood, squander but the time
Of one short day in folly and the crime
Of idleness, and let thy spirit rust
With luxury and sloth, and let the dust
Of rude and hot dissensions gather o'er
Thy energies. the moth of passion score
Thy heart with seams,—mark how the light will
    frown,
And how the lustrous stars will glimmer down
In sorrow ; not a flower upon the glade
That does its mission that will not upbraid
Thy faithlessness ; the trees and flowers will seem
To look upon thee with reproach ; the stream
Will shape its murmurs into words of scorn,
That thou, a man, in God's own image born.
Of all his works the finish, should descend
To be most faithless to his beginning's end.

Why, then, should we amid our labor stand
With folded arms, mere idlers in the land?
Why say, because of little use appears
The noiseless movement of our silent years.
Our life is useless, and our work too low,
Our bound too narrow and our step too slow?
Distils the dew, and doth the summer rain
Fall on the leaves and on the flowers in vain?
The rill that creeps beside the travelled way,—
The grass is greener where its waters play!
And doth the oak prove faithless to its end,
Because no blossoms from its branches bend?
And doth the frailest little wood-flower fail
Because it shadows not one-half the vale?
No, never! bending grass and creeping vine,
The dullest worm, the feeblest stars that shine,
Fail not ; nor fails the man whose steps pursue
The path that lies along his earnest view,
However narrow, with the patient tread,
That always marks the faithful traveller, led
By all-enduring patience, and the zeal
That faith and hope and honest purpose feel.
Truth's stern apostles, in the old times fought
With ignorance and error, till they wrought,
With such made weapons as their hands could find,
Great revolutions in an Age's mind.
No matter where they labored, where they worked,
Or in what den or in what desert lurked ;
No matter who approved or who said no,
Who bade them welcome or who bade them go.—
They did their work, nor for a moment turned,

Though edicts thundered and though faggots
    burned.
And did they fail because the rusted lock,
The glittering axe, the cruel cross, the block,
Cramped their strong limbs and drank their
    streaming gore,
Ere half the labor of their work was o'er?
Fail? now the world stands stoutly up to bless
Those brave old heroes, and the hardiness
'And stern unyielding strength with which they
    strove
To do their mission: and although they clove
With ponderous blows, but here and there a bar,
And opened but the bolted door ajar,
Through which the slightest thread of light stole
    in;
Yet nobly in their time did they begin
The conquest which the arm of after-strength
Pursued triumphant, till the door at length
Was thrown wide open, and the noonday sun
Streamed in to finish what they had begun.
Then, see thou prove thyself a man, and seek
To do, from day to day, from week to week,
The work that falleth to thy hands, aright.
Let the still evening and the morning light
Find thee about thy mission; murmuring not
With childish humor at thy brother's lot,
Nor wondering why thy duty was not shown
To do some other mission than thine own;
Not doubting if thy labor or thine art
With its dull toil be not thy neighbor's part;

Nor questioning why thou with want art pressed,
While sits thy neighbor in his linen dressed;
Nor shirking off thy task with cunning skill;
Nor shrinking from its toil with coward will,—
But bravely working on as best thou can,
And standing to thy duty like a man,—
Whether thy mission here shall prove to be
To dig, from morn till night, in penury,
With sunburnt hands and never-ceasing toil,
Thy scanty living from the torpid soil;
To do thy work with—'spite the scorn of fools—
The stout mechanic's honorable tools;
To move with mammon in the bustling mart;
To ply the chisel or the brush of art;
To travel in the scholar's quiet ways;
To feel thy being quicken in the rays
Of eagle-visioned science,—manfully
Fulfil that mission, though thou canst not see
Its import, or divine the use or end
To which its strange and various changes tend.
And when, at length, upon thy work all done,
Gleams the last radiance of life's setting sun,
As slowly down, with bright unclouded face,
Behind the glowing hills he sinks apace,
The glory of a life well spent shall shed
Its softened influence on thy honored head,
Wreathe round thy pillow while the heavens are
    stilled,
And crown thy mission faithfully fulfilled.

www.ingramcontent.com/pod-product-compliance
Lightning Source LLC
Chambersburg PA
CBHW021409230426
43666CB00006B/680